STRATEGY JOURNEYS

Strategy Journeys starts from the premise that strategic planning suffers from a bad press: it can be seen as complex, technical, remote from the day-to-day reality of an organisation, undertaken by an elite specialist executive group, producing threatening changes whose rationale is barely understood – or, perhaps worse still, having no worthwhile impact at all.

For many senior executives, strategic planning is too daunting a task, which is why they often seek help from those with the expertise to guide the process: they have a severe lack of confidence in their own ability to design, plan and implement such an important and major project.

Yet organisations have never had greater need for a flexible, resilient and engaging approach to strategic planning than now. How do those leading an organisation know where to start, what approach to take and how to go about the process of strategic planning? David Booth aims to help them by demystifying the concept and propounding a 'first principles' approach to developing a strategic plan within the context of the individual organisation and with the flexibility to adapt the process to focus on what really matters. He suggests the key questions that should be asked when considering embarking on a strategic planning 'journey' to help design and guide the process.

David Booth has over 20 years of business management experience working for companies such as United Biscuits, Grand Metropolitan and Smith & Nephew, in marketing and then HR and strategic development at the senior management level, followed by working for the past 16 years as an independent management consultant helping organisations with their 'strategy journeys': clients include a range of large and medium-sized organisations from international financial services companies to specialist NHS Foundation Trusts. These projects have involved working intensively with client organisations, guiding and complementing their internal knowledge and resources to help steer their strategic planning processes and develop effective strategic plans: there has been a strong emphasis on organisational learning, and clients have remarked on the continuing value and relevance of the work.

STRATEGY JOURNEYS

A guide to effective strategic planning

David Booth

Routledge
Taylor & Francis Group

LONDON AND NEW YORK

First published 2017
by Routledge
2 Park Square, Milton Park, Abingdon, Oxon OX14 4RN

and by Routledge
711 Third Avenue, New York, NY 10017

Routledge is an imprint of the Taylor & Francis Group, an informa business

British Library Cataloguing in Publication Data
A catalogue record for this book is available from the British Library

Library of Congress Cataloging-in-Publication Data
A catalog record for this book has been requested.

ISBN: 978-1-409-46559-1 (hbk)
ISBN: 978-1-138-69676-1 (pbk)
ISBN: 978-1-315-61101-3 (ebk)

Typeset in Sabon
by Apex CoVantage, LLC

MIX
Paper from
responsible sources
FSC® C013985
www.fsc.org

Printed in the United Kingdom
by Henry Ling Limited

CONTENTS

List of figures   vii
List of tables   ix

Introduction   1

PART I
What is strategic planning?   5

1 A brief history   7

2 Demystifying strategic planning   12

3 The heart of strategic planning   20

PART II
How to develop a strategic plan   **31**

4 Why develop a strategic plan?   33

5 The process   43

6 The content   61

7 The story   86

PART III
What makes an effective strategic plan?   **93**

8 Engagement   95

9 Implementation   102

10 Review   114

      Epilogue: the maths and music of strategic planning   120

      Bibliography   122
      Index   123

FIGURES

2.1	What's in a name?	14
2.2	The external context	15
2.3	The internal context	16
2.4	The process	17
2.5	Context, process, content	18
3.1	Organisational energy	22
3.2	The four stages	23
3.3	Strategising and organising	24
3.4	Strategic planning: the principal activities	24
3.5	Strategic planning as sensemaking	27
3.6	Rich conversations	28
4.1	Why develop a strategic plan?	35
4.2	The lifecycle of a strategic plan	39
4.3	Refreshing the strategic plan	39
4.4	Realised versus intended strategy	40
4.5	Changing contexts	42
5.1	Framing the challenge	45
5.2	Involving stakeholders	47
5.3	Planning the journey	49
5.4	Where are we now?	50
5.5	Asking the questions	50
5.6	Intensity and focus	52
5.7	Objectives of meetings	53
5.8	Coordinating workstreams	54
5.9	Workstream paths	58
6.1	Information and insights (the hidden depths of data)	66
6.2	SWOT	67
6.3	Boston Consulting Group portfolio analysis matrix	68
6.4	Risk assessment grid	68
6.5	Evaluating 'What if . . .?'	76
6.6	Projections perspectives	77
6.7	Projection model	78
6.8	Linked projection model	79
6.9	Scenarios	82

6.10	Organisational performance	83
6.11	Predictable-control grid	83
6.12	Assessing risks	84
6.13	Risk mitigation	85
7.1	Argument flows	88
7.2	Developing the themes	91
7.3	Organising strategic initiatives	92
8.1	Steps to commitment	97
8.2	Agreement and understanding	97
8.3	Organisational ownership	98
8.4	Purpose, values and principles	100
8.5	Platform for action	101
9.1	Sustaining organisational energy	104
9.2	Strategic initiatives and operational activities	106
9.3	Change energy model	107
9.4	Strategic measures	109
9.5	Strategic Scorecard	110
9.6	Strategic plan as system	112
10.1	Organisational alertness	116
10.2	Strategy journeys	118
10.3	Strategic planning	119

TABLES

2.1   Strategic planning alternative terms   13
3.1   Answering the question   21
5.1   Reasons for developing a strategic plan   44

INTRODUCTION

Why write this book?

'Strategic planning': two words that provoke a variety of responses, from the dread of months of extra work, distraction from the 'real' job and postponed decisions, to apprehension about yet more imposed change. Strategic planning suffers from several perceptions. It can be seen as complex, technical, remote from the day-to-day reality of an organisation, undertaken by an elite internal group or external management consultants, producing threatening changes whose rationale is barely understood – or, perhaps worse, having no worthwhile impact at all. In today's fast-changing world, where adaptability and rapid responses are often championed as the keys to business survival, it is easy to see why investing valuable organisational resources and energy in developing detailed 'five-year plans' might not be considered a priority. Perhaps strategic planning is no longer relevant?

And yet over the past 50 years strategic planning has become established as a 'best practice' management discipline, supported by business school teaching and research and championed by management consultancies. Schools of strategic planning have developed, become fashionable and then faded, and theories, tools and techniques have all evolved. In the world of management, 'strategy' has kudos, implying importance, influence and therefore power. Strategic planning has been invested with weight – substance (mass) multiplied by seriousness (gravity) – so there's an edifice of reputation to demystify.

For many senior executives, strategic planning is too daunting a task, which is why they often seek help from those with the expertise to guide the process. They have a severe lack of confidence in their own ability to design, plan and implement such an important and major project. And for those asked to help develop their organisation's strategic plan, a not uncommon first reaction is to ask how – what information, what format, who do I involve, how do I go about it?

There is of course a wealth of published books and articles to help them, as well as some well-known strategic analysis tools many managers will be familiar with from their MBA courses. Classic textbooks like Johnson and Scholes[1] cover a comprehensive range of techniques; Mintzberg[2] describes eloquently how the different approaches to strategic planning have developed over time; Porter[3] focuses on industry structure, whilst Hamel and Prahalad[4] champion a competency-led approach to strategy, and Gratton[5] a people-led perspective, with Stacey's[6] complexity theory resonating with the uncertainties of today's fast-changing markets and environment.

Another approach might be to try to copy the style of other organisations' strategic plans, replicating the content of impressive-looking documents, or to adopt a standard 'template', faithfully completing each section almost as a 'painting by numbers' exercise. With thoughtful adaptation this might work – but it is in the adaptation rather than the adoption that the skill lies in developing a strategic plan that is appropriate for that organisation at that time and that engages its people and motivates action.

But despite such accessible knowledge, how do those leading an organisation know where to start, what approach to take and how to go about the process of strategic planning in a way that is right for their organisation? This book aims to help them by demystifying the concept and propounding a 'first principles' approach to developing a strategic plan within the context of an individual organisation and with the flexibility to adapt the process to focus on what really matters to the organisation. It suggests some of the questions that should be asked when considering embarking on a strategic planning 'journey' to help design and guide the process.

In writing this book I have drawn on my 20 years' experience of helping organisations develop strategic plans, working with them on all aspects from strategy development to planning to implementation. I have always been driven by wanting to understand things, questioning until I get to the underlying reasons or core principles involved. In my career this manifested itself as a tendency to think strategically, to try and get to the heart of the issue – and a thirst for learning and broadening my knowledge. When I first became involved in strategic planning, my impression was of a grand, authoritative and complicated process resulting in a definitive and encyclopaedic exposition of how an organisation fits into its market and how it was going to ensure its future success. How impressive were the insightful analyses, slick charts and persuasive arguments presented by the leading management consultancies, engaged to help the corporate head office define the future direction (often requiring a major corporate restructure . . .)! But I was fortunate to have experienced a few occasions when persistent questioning exposed flaws beneath the gloss, when deeper probing challenged the assumptions and conclusions that were presented so persuasively, helping me realise that all that glistens is not always gold. It's neither the sophistication of the analysis nor the style of the presentation that matter so much as insight and understanding – and the process by which those are achieved.

There is one formative experience that stands out that helped define my approach to strategic planning. I was part of the executive team formed to establish a major new division of a large international company, and as the team got to work the cry went up: 'We need a strategic plan!' External help was sought, and a parade of management consultancies presented their recommendations – from detailed project plans to outline document formats – and a stack of proposal documents and handouts built up in the file. But one person walked into the boardroom with just a blank sheet of paper and asked, 'So what precisely do you want to achieve?' Out of the ensuing discussion came the realisation that – despite the agreed formal brief – those in the room had widely differing views about the new organisation. More talking, and some listening. Another blank piece of paper – this time flipchart sized – and a marker pen. Discussion, clarification, differences. The 30-minute 'credentials and presentation' slot became two hours of intense communication, at the end of which there was a simple sketched flipchart diagram mapping out how we were going to begin to address some of the issues. The organisation's strategy journey had started, not as a result of some grand plan, but from people talking and – importantly – listening, to achieve a common understanding of the challenges and how they were going to work together to address them.

A word (or two)

This formative experience taught me that creating a strategic plan is not about applying standard methods and processes, progressing step-by-step to a predefined timetable and writing up the results. The process for each organisation is different, beginning from a unique starting point along an individual path to develop what is most relevant and appropriate for that particular organisation at that specific time – with decisions along the way as to how to progress. Hence I have used the term 'strategy journeys', which seems to me to convey the exploration and adventure involved – and it captures how an organisation thinks, decides, communicates and adapts as it works out where it wants to go and how it's going to get there. We will examine further some of the terminology associated with strategy development and strategic planning in chapters 2 and 3.

Throughout this book I use the term 'organisation' rather than 'business or 'company'. This is because strategic planning is relevant not just to commercial, profit-making companies, whether they are established multi-national corporations or small start-up enterprises. The challenge of working out where to get to and how to get there can apply to any group of people organised around a common purpose, including public sector, non-profit, voluntary groups, social enterprises, and academic and professional institutions. 'Organisation' includes this whole spectrum.

There is also liberal use of metaphors, analogies and other language devices to help describe and explain ideas. Strategic planning straddles both the business and academic fields, and the terminology can readily become dry and distant, yet the principles and approach are in essence straightforward and rational, and my aim in this book is to bring these to life and help them be understood by a wider audience. Different styles of learning work for different people; I hope that for many readers of this book my attempts to stimulate images, pictures and ideas in their minds will help make these ideas accessible and understandable.

For similar reasons there are a lot of diagrams. In my work with organisations helping them develop their strategic plans I am often pleasantly surprised at how effective a diagram can be in conveying ideas and information and so helping achieve shared understanding; diagrams can crystallise the thinking in a way words might struggle to achieve.

Who will benefit?

The book is written for senior managers and executives who are likely to be leading or involved in strategic planning within their organisations – either now or in the near future – and who are looking for an approach that will help their overall understanding of strategic planning and how to undertake this effectively. The emphasis is on what to consider when thinking about developing a strategic plan, what process might be appropriate and what might help with this. I have avoided too deep an exploration of theory, which is better covered by more academic publications; in addition, I have not covered the impressive array of tools and techniques that can help with strategic analysis but that can also contribute to the often-associated impression of complexity and sophistication. Such tools and techniques are already more than adequately covered in other, excellent books, and my aim in this book is to show how strategic planning is really about answering some simple, fundamental questions, and hence not the exclusive preserve of experts.

Why is it different?

There are many excellent books and stimulating research papers about strategic planning, and some of the techniques used in strategic analysis and the evaluation of strategic options will be familiar to senior managers from MBAs and other business courses. However, whilst these might equip executives with the tools, the challenge of how to design, organise and steer a strategic planning process is at a different level of strategic leadership. This book aims to help people think about how to approach such a challenge and to give them the confidence to think through some of the issues involved.

The structure of the book

The book is organised in three sections. Part I explores 'What is strategic planning?' beginning with a brief summary of the thinking that has developed about the formation of strategy over the past 50 years. The next two chapters then aim to demystify strategic planning and to focus on what it is really about. Part II looks at some of the practical aspects of developing a strategic plan, including understanding why the organisation is choosing to undertake this at a particular time. We will explore the process of developing a strategic plan, the knowledge and understanding that is developed during that process and how this is captured and used. Finally, Part III examines some of the factors that make an effective strategic plan, including how it is implemented.

The approach taken within each chapter is to use examples and case studies to help illustrate topics where appropriate. Diagrams and tables are included liberally to help summarise and break up the text for interest and readability (my experience of developing strategic plans with organisations has demonstrated the power of diagrams to crystallise information and aid understanding). References are included in the text, and the bibliography lists a selection of books to help the reader follow up and explore further any topics that might be of particular interest.

Notes

1   Johnson G., Scholes K. and Whittington R., *Exploring Corporate Strategy* (7th edition), Financial Times Prentice Hall, Harlow, UK, 2006
2   Mintzberg H., Ahlstrand B. and Lampel J., *Strategy Safari*, Financial Times Prentice Hall, Harlow, UK, 1998
3   Porter M., *Competitive Strategy*, Free Press, New York, 1980
4   Hamel G. and Prahalad C., *Competing for the Future*, Harvard Business School, Boston, 1994
5   Gratton L., *Living Strategy*, Financial Times Prentice Hall, Harlow, UK, 2000
6   Stacey R., *Strategic Management and Organisational Dynamics* (5th edition), Financial Times Prentice Hall, Harlow, UK, 2007

Part I

WHAT IS STRATEGIC PLANNING?

1

A BRIEF HISTORY

People have always been fascinated with strategy. It implies a degree of mastery – of the ability to outwit others and influence outcomes, to determine the future. There is the appeal of intellectual challenge, the competitiveness of playing to win, the exercise of power, the satisfaction of achievement – it's like a game of chess (although the pieces are far from wooden) or deploying the forces at your disposal to win the war. Lessons derived from military strategists from Sun Tzu to Bonaparte, von Clausewitz and Montgomery are consumed avidly by organisational leaders in their search for insights, and the language of seeking advantage permeates many boardroom discussions about strategy.

But strategy also implies the need to think things through, to seek to understand a situation and articulate the options clearly, to discuss, debate and decide with others and act accordingly. It relates to how organisations function, their styles and cultures, how decisions are made, how change happens – all aspects of learning how to be an effective leader, how to motivate people and how to inspire an organisation to future success.

In an organisational context, are strategies determined as a result of a deliberate process of analysis, applying best practice techniques and the lessons learnt from business school case studies to plan out how an organisation can best compete? Or do they evolve from within the organisation as people learn from what develops and the views they form about its strengths and opportunities?

Part of the fascination with strategic planning is how it encompasses such differing approaches to the development of strategy, and there is an innate tension in the juxtaposition of the words 'strategic' and 'planning' that we will explore later in the book. It brings together the logic of analysis with the complexities of organisations and combines academic theory with practical application.

It is also fair to point out that it has attained a certain cachet. To be involved in strategic planning implies either the ability for high-level thinking about complex issues, or the ability to influence fundamental decisions in the organisation, or both. But – as I shall argue later in this chapter – the period of 'specialness' and 'exclusivity' of skills related to strategic planning is now over; whilst expertise and knowledge are still essential, the opportunities to acquire that understanding are broadening, and more people are able to participate and contribute in an organisation's strategy journey with confidence rather than with trepidation. At the same time, there is much being learnt – and much still to learn – about the relationship of people with organisations, the dynamics of how organisations work, how the health of the organisation can be as vital for its longer-term success as its current performance. I hope that this book – which adopts a common-sense, first principles approach to what really matters in developing an effective strategic plan – will contribute in at least a small way to helping others develop the confidence to participate with enthusiasm in the challenge of shaping their organisation's future.

In the beginning

Whereas 'strategy' might have its linguistic origins and first military associations rooted in Greek and Chinese literature from the sixth and fifth centuries B.C., strategic planning as a concept is less than a hundred years old. Indeed, it was not until the 1920s that a strategic planning business model first appeared – perhaps as a result of the economic retrenchment following the First World War affecting the growth prospects of the large-scale commercial organisations that had developed through extensive world-wide trading opportunities following the Industrial Revolution. This was the Harvard Policy Model developed by Harvard Business School as a planning methodology for private businesses. But it was another 40 years before strategic planning as a defined concept started to gain wider recognition; from the late 1960s onwards the profile and adoption of strategic planning increased rapidly, both within businesses and academically. Professional societies and networks for practitioners were established, such as the Strategic Planning Society (1967) and the Strategic Management Society (1981), which both started in London. In the 1990s more public sector organisations introduced strategic planning as 'best organisational practice'.

So strategic planning has a relatively recent history as an established practice widely adopted by organisations and informed by academic study. However, there has been significant development over these 50 years in both the theory and practice of strategic planning. Henry Mintzberg[1] has identified 10 schools of thought that have developed over this time, which he describes simply and engagingly in his books: I could not hope to do justice to them, but in this chapter I will attempt a brief summary (which I hope will whet the appetite of readers interested in exploring these further), together with some personal observations.

The schools of strategic planning

The first schools of thought sought to map out how organisations should go about the process of formulating strategy. The *Design* school that developed in the 1960s set out an approach that still forms a useful process template today: an initial stage of analysing the organisation's situation from an external and internal perspective, including identifying its strengths and weaknesses and the opportunities and threats in its environment. Key factors for success were compared with the organisation's distinctive competences to help formulate strategy options for evaluation; when a strategy had been chosen the organisation then started to implement that strategy.

This was a methodical process that organisations could adopt as a 'top-down' instigated initiative and that they could work through logically. It was designed to produce a clearly defined and fully formulated strategy specific to the organisation, which it would then implement, based on the premise that the organisation would be able to bring together information that would enable it to form a clear assessment of its external and internal situation.

The approach of deliberately setting out to develop a strategic plan led to the emergence of the *Planning* school, which became widely adopted in the 1970s. This was the time when 'Corporate Planning Departments' became popular in larger organisations to coordinate a stage-by-stage planning process across divisions or departments. It involved a very controlled and structured approach, with clear delineation of responsibilities, often as part of an annual planning process (first agree on your strategic plan, then your annual plan is based on the first year of implementing this, with budget-setting following to a phased timetable set across the organisational hierarchy). Strategic options would be analysed rigorously by the Corporate Planning team, and these strategies decided which options the divisions or departments would implement according to defined plans. Such an approach led to the distancing of the corporate planning expertise from the organisation's business units and a consequent lack of ownership. Typically this resulted in a financially dominated evaluation process, with mergers, acquisitions and disposals a frequent outcome in larger corporations.

The 1980s saw the development of another very influential school of strategic planning. This focused on working out the optimum strategic *Positioning* of the organisation to gain competitive advantage based on thorough analysis and assessment, at industry and market levels, of the forces influencing these and the value chain of the organisation. The emphasis on analysis and the use of techniques and templates to assess the results led to a boom in management consultancies providing strategic planning expertise to help organisations, both by specialist teams within the large international consultancy/accounting firms and by the boutique 'strategy consultancies' that developed during this period. The reliance on what became standard analysis-informed frameworks for deciding the optimum strategic position – and hence strategy – for the organisation to adopt resulted in these strategies often being generic; the analysis of information was more sophisticated, but unlike the Design school this did not necessarily lead to a strategy uniquely tailored to the organisation considered as a whole, and as with the Planning school important elements of the development of the strategic plan were entrusted to others outside the immediate organisation.

These three schools were based on the premise that organisations chose to initiate the formulation of their strategies and that this was a deliberate decision requiring a defined structured process using tried and tested techniques. But during the 1980s and 1990s the thinking of some of those involved in strategic planning academically or as practitioners started to turn towards how strategies were formed in practice, rather than how they were intended to be formed, and this led to six more schools of thought.

The *Entrepreneurial* school recognised the influence of visionary leaders or business founders in deciding the future direction of development of their organisations. Frequently strategies developed almost semiconsciously in the mind of the leader based on what he or she felt were opportunities for the business; these could be vaguely formed initially, but would be refined as the ideas crystallised. The strategic opportunity could involve a leap by the organisation into new areas and involve significant risk – but it was the personal judgement of the leader and his or her championing of the strategy that would lead to its adoption.

The *Cognitive* school considered the mental processes by which people develop strategy. It looked at how creating a conceptual map can help people come to an interpretation of a situation and how constructing mental frameworks helps put various elements in perspective and provide a structure for their thinking. It is a way of articulating the situation as perceived and understood.

The value of organisational awareness and learning were reflected in the *Learning* school. Strategies emerge from the organisation's experience and the signals provided by its environment; the organisation's own actions can help shape these, with an understanding forming incrementally of the strategy that is 'right' for the organisation as people try to make sense of their situation. This school lends itself to an experimental approach, where ideas are tried by the organisation and strategies are shaped depending on what is learnt; there is a risk of ineffective strategies evolving and of organisations experiencing 'strategic drift' away from successful strategies.

The *Power* school views strategic planning as a negotiation process, as a competition for the organisation's resources based on the political processes of influence and building alliances. This can occur on two levels: within the organisation in order to influence decisions and externally as the organisation strengthens its position through formal or informal ventures with others. Strategy is shaped by persuasion and bargaining.

The importance of organisational culture in influencing strategy is reflected in the *Cultural* school. Strategy formation is a process of social interaction based on the beliefs and perspectives within the organisation, what people understand about their organisation and its role in relation to others and what it is capable of doing. The risk of this approach is that there might be insufficient challenge and stimulus within the process from new ideas or perspectives and the need to consider more radical opportunities to develop.

The thinking of the *Environmental* school is based on the need for the organisation to adapt to its environment and focuses on developing the strategic capabilities to respond effectively. It is a somewhat reactive approach to strategy formation, and whilst the ability to assess changes in the organisation's environment and make fast decisions is desirable, there is a risk that the ability of the organisation to make choices that will influence its environment will be underplayed.

The last of the 10 schools that Mintzberg describes, the *Configuration* school, is based on the premise that the right strategic planning process for an organisation depends on its situation at that time. Each of the approaches of the other schools has merits when used appropriately, and there are stages in the life of an organisation when these might be relevant. Different strategy approaches are required during times of major change compared to periods of greater stability, and the emphases within strategy formation and strategic planning will change accordingly.

Adopting the lessons

The development of these schools of strategic planning has broadened and deepened understanding about how strategy develops in organisations and some of the approaches that can be adopted. They reflect a variety of emphases: the logical assessment of an organisation's situation and consequent formulation of strategy; the need to coordinate the process across different parts of an organisation; the value of analysis and tools to interpret it; how leadership and vision influence an organisation's strategy; how people and organisations make sense of their situation; the role influence and negotiation can play in determining strategy; how cultural beliefs influence strategy; the need to adapt to changes in the environment; and the fact that any of these approaches might be applicable to an organisation at various times in its lifetime.

For me, one of the most valuable benefits of understanding these different perspectives is to realise that strategic planning has many facets; there is a depth and breadth that is thought provoking. The challenge of applying this thinking to help an organisation develop its strategic plan requires considering the unique situation of that organisation – the approach that is right for it at this time might not be appropriate for other organisations, or even for that organisation at a different time.

It also reinforces my belief that the best approach to strategic planning is to consider it from a first principles perspective, based on the fundamentals of what it really is about, followed by an appreciation of these various aspects and different approaches to work out what process is right for that organisation at that particular time. This book is based on that philosophy and the belief that such an approach to strategic planning, demystifying it and working from simple basic principles, is one that can be understood and adopted by anyone in an organisation and hence that strategic planning is not the preserve of a select few.

Note

1   Mintzberg H., Ahlstrand B. and Lampel J., *Strategy Safari*, Financial Times Prentice Hall, Harlow, UK, 1998

2

DEMYSTIFYING STRATEGIC PLANNING

Fundamentals and first principles: basic questions and the art of conversation

As we saw in the last chapter, strategic planning has evolved through several models and approaches. But rather than expend a lot of time and energy worrying about what might be the latest trends in academic thinking, consultancy best practice or leading companies' approaches, I should like to step back and start from first principles to consider how strategy is formed.

Understanding the fundamentals is a healthy foundation for effective strategic planning; it will help instil the confidence to decide on the right approach for an organisation, to learn and adopt ideas from others and to adapt the process and guide that organisation's particular strategy journey.

Learning mathematics provides a useful analogy. Those who have a firm grasp of the underlying concepts are in a much stronger position to apply this to new problems, compared to others who rely on a 'learned-by-rote' procedure. So, for example, children who are taught a particular method for solving a problem without understanding why it produces the correct answer will struggle to adapt to new techniques or to apply their knowledge to unfamiliar situations outside their experience.

The aim of this chapter is to pare strategic planning to the simple elements that are at its heart.

What's in a name?

I've always struggled with the term 'strategic planning'. It sounds analytical, dry and remote – and also somewhat self-important, with the traditional image of an almost elitist activity done 'for' (and often 'to') the people in an organisation by a specialist corporate team or external consultants.

'Strategic planning' also invokes impressions of a deliberate, structured process, which to some would seem late-twentieth-century fashion. In recent years the thinking is that strategy 'emerges' in the learning organisation, whilst for others it is their rapid-response adaptability and 'trial and error' approach that enable them to seize market opportunities and tactically outflank their competitors. It's time perhaps for a new name which leaves behind the stereotype of 'traditional' strategic planning and reflects a more dynamic approach. So what term should we use?

Table 2.1 Strategic planning alternative terms

Strategic management	Taking responsibility for shaping, implementing and achieving the organisation's strategy
Strategic leadership	Setting the direction for how the organisation develops
Strategy development	The process by which an organisation determines and articulates its strategy
Strategic learning	Increasing the organisation's ability to develop and implement an appropriate strategy by reflecting on recent experience
Strategic development	Making significant progress as an organisation through the implementation of agreed-upon strategic initiatives
Strategic planning	The process by which an organisation determines and articulates its strategy and how it intends to achieve it

Considering some of the terms in Table 2.1, each has different emphases:

- *Strategic Management* is one of the terms that seems to be preferred more recently – it gives an impression of an ongoing process of corporate responsibility, continual review and progressive change, ensuring the organisation achieves its goals. But this can also give the perception that this is an executive-level corporate responsibility; it doesn't convey the importance of engagement and ownership throughout the organisation or the discovery and emergence of strategy by doing and listening.
- *Strategic Leadership* incorporates the dynamism of the *L* buzzword – but with the danger of responsibility residing even higher in the hierarchy pyramid than for the term 'strategic management'.
- *Strategy Development* does not encompass the important aspect of implementation – the specifics of who, what, how and when (the where and the why having been decided by the strategy development process).
- *Strategic Learning* is inward looking and does not express adequately the need to take decisions and act, to bring about something new and better (for example, what's the practical impact on the organisation and its customers?).
- *Strategic Development* reflects thinking, learning, growth plus practical implementation. Strategic development = developing strategy + making strategy happen + moving forward as an organisation. It thus includes the key dynamic elements of effective strategic planning. However, it also gives the impression of significant change, which is not always the outcome of a strategic plan; nor does the strategic development of an organisation depend on strategic planning.

Part of the problem lies in the combination of the two words, 'strategic' and 'planning'. 'Strategic' implies long-term, conceptual, directional, requiring deep thinking from a 'higher-level' perspective – the consideration of hypothetical scenarios, theoretical options and their possible implications. 'Planning', on the other hand, is associated with near-future, operational detail resulting in almost-immediate action – the 'who, what and when' rather than the 'what if' and 'why'. From this interpretation, the skills involved in developing strategy would seem to be very different from those required in a planning process.

13

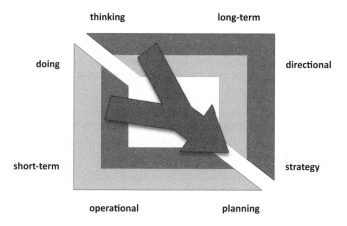

thinking long-term

doing directional

short-term strategy

operational planning

Figure 2.1 What's in a name?

Yet perhaps it is this juxtaposition of terms that reinforces that strategic planning is about *both* the thinking and the action, the longer-term opportunities but also the immediate steps required to achieve these. It is the combination of both strategy formulation and action planning, with a specific end purpose in mind, that maps strategic planning's position in the plethora of 'strategic' terms.

This might also be one of the reasons strategic planning is perceived as being somewhat daunting, requiring the weaving together of these different skills and mindsets in a cohesive way. And the challenge for those working out how to go about strategic planning is how to orchestrate this successfully.

The three dimensions

Understandably, most focus is usually placed on the end result of strategic planning: the glossy document complete with preface signed by the chair and chief executive replete with an impressively comprehensive set of appendices. After months of input from all departments, board workshops and numerous drafts and redrafts, the final Strategic Plan document is at last signed off by the board just in time to meet the group head office's corporate deadline (or that of the external regulator). Boxes ticked, it is proudly championed as setting out in detail the way forward for the organisation for the next five years, taking pride of place on the chief executive's office shelf (at least for a while).

Although there is more than a hint of slightly mocking stereotyping in this description, unfortunately it is not without justification in some cases, influencing commonly held perceptions about strategic planning.

It is easy to see why so much attention is focused on the strategic plan document itself. It is the tangible output from all the work and effort that has been put in, usually over several months, and it captures the important decisions that have been made about the organisation's future. But as we shall see, there are other dimensions to strategic planning that are also very relevant and potentially as valuable.

Another common approach to strategic planning is to try to adopt a template format for the strategic plan document. On several occasions I have been asked at the start of a strategic planning process to define what the final document will look like; I have also come across instances where a format for the document has been specified and the various parts of the organisation tasked to complete allocated sections – a 'paint-by-numbers' approach to compiling what should aspire to be a coherent and inspiring picture of a desirable future. Of course it is understandable that people are keen to form a picture of what the final result might look like: it can help them work out what they might need to do and how they can best contribute – and there are ways of describing an outline framework and approach that can help them do this. However, as we shall see, every organisation is different, with its own particular issues and opportunities, capabilities and potential, and each organisation must work out for itself how these might affect its future and what is the most appropriate way for it to address these.

There are three dimensions to considering how to develop an effective strategic plan.

First is the *context* in which this is to take place. This includes both the current situation of the organisation in its wider environment and its internal state and organisational health. The external context will reflect:

- The *scope* of the strategic plan: the market territory (e.g., geographical area) and the range of customer needs (products and services) which the organisation should consider at this time
- The *contours* in this territory: the players (e.g., competitors, regulators) exerting influence and shaping the 'gravitational field' affecting others
- The *dynamics* at play: what's changing, and what is likely to change (the trends and potential game-changers).

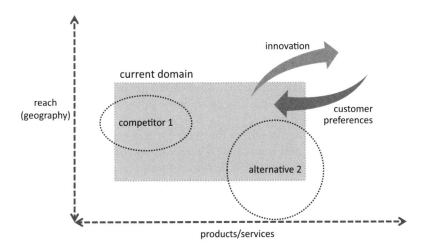

Figure 2.2 The external context

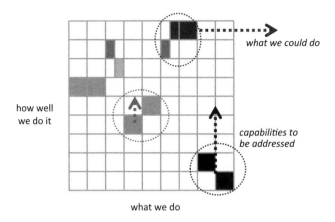

Figure 2.3 The internal context

The internal state of the organisation will also influence where attention is likely to be directed during the strategic planning process, such as what isn't working well and what capabilities the organisation has that could be developed and applied in different ways.

The second dimension to developing a strategic plan is the *process*:

- Who should be involved, what do they need to do and how will they go about doing this? How will the work be organised, what resources will be required and which of these will be dedicated solely to this?
- Who are the stakeholders, and what is their role in this process? By whom and how will decisions be made? Who will contribute, and who needs to approve the outcome? Are there formal requirements, either internal procedures or external reviews, that need to be taken into account?
- Over what time scale will this take place, and what are the milestones along the way? What should be the style and pace of this process? For example, is it better to allow the thinking to develop and be refined, or does the context require a more defined project management approach?
- How will the outputs be captured? What needs to be recorded formally? Are stages completed sequentially, or is an iterative approach with continual refinement more appropriate?
- What should be communicated as the work progresses, to whom and when – upwards, downwards and outwards? There will be contexts in which confidentiality is paramount, for example if sensitive options are being explored; in other circumstances sharing the thinking and ideas as they develop can be helpful in developing wider understanding and encouraging contributions.

Content is the third dimension when considering developing a strategic plan:

- Are there any specific requirements for the format of the output(s) or what is included? For example, do any external stakeholders (corporate or regulatory)

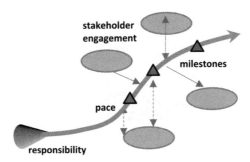

Figure 2.4 The process

specify what information they need and how it should be presented so that they can collate with others' plans?

- Whilst the focus is commonly on a final strategic plan document, there might be other outputs developed during the process that are useful for the organisation.
- Different versions of a strategic plan might be appropriate for different audiences (for example, summaries of the key points, or public vs. internal), and sections might be developed in more detail for various groups (departments, subsidiaries, functions) to help them contribute to the organisation achieving its strategic plan.
- How complete and finished is the strategic planning process when a particular output is developed? Is it compiling a comprehensive set of plans for the organisation, or is it more capturing 'work in progress' as a platform for the next stage?
- What style is most appropriate for any outputs? Comprehensive and detailed, with lots of supporting information, or setting out directions and high-level themes and initiatives? Should the tone be inspiring people to think through what they need to do or instructional and setting out specific actions and targets?

Context, process and *content* – thinking about each of these three dimensions is important when considering how to go about developing a strategic plan. In our strategy journey analogy, *context* is 'the view from here', *process* is the route that is planned and *content* is what is discovered and experienced along the way. We shall return to these and explore them in more depth in part 2. Keeping these in mind as the work progresses will help adapt the process and modify expectations of the outcomes to reflect what has been learnt or any changes in the context. This is all part of the art of effective strategic planning.

Three questions

So far in this chapter we have considered some of the tensions inherent in the term 'strategic planning', the need to combine different types of thinking and perspectives and the three dimensions involved in developing a strategic plan. But what is its purpose, what role does a strategic plan play and what is its contribution to an organisation? In short, we have yet to actually *define* strategic planning.

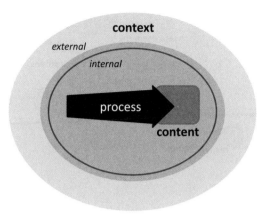

Figure 2.5 Context, process, content

As I was writing this book, at this point I was faced with a choice. The strategist in me was straining at the leash to undertake an academic literature review, to explore the various definitions of 'strategy' and 'strategic' and discuss their strengths and limitations and to develop a hierarchy of the scope, organisational breadth and time perspective of plans and then to bring these together triumphantly into a neat, universally applicable definition of strategic planning. However intellectually appealing such a discourse might be, essentially it would be a diversion from the principal purpose of this book, which is to act as a more practical guide to those involved in developing strategic plans for their organisations. The academic theorising will have to wait for another time!

Instead I will jump straight to a simple working definition of strategic planning:

> *Strategic planning is the process by which an organisation decides where it wants to go and how it's going to get there.*

I will introduce some refinements to this later; however, this initial working draft includes some of the fundamental aspects of strategic planning: first, that it's a *process*; second, that it involves identifying an intended *path*; third, that it involves making *decisions*; and fourth, that it requires the organisation to work out *how* it is going to try to reach that destination. The inclusion of the word 'and' in the definition is essential to ensure a focus on practical implementation as well as strategic intentions.

One of the advantages of this working definition is how it places the emphasis on the process, rather than a document (as we shall see later, this is a shift in mindset that has important implications). It also states clearly the purpose of strategic planning, which is an organisation determining its desired future. And this definition is quite broad in its scope and application; it doesn't specify the type of process or who should be involved. So the decision-making process can encompass engaging stakeholders, obtaining regulatory approval, formal board agreement and gaining the commitment of the people working in the organisation, whatever is appropriate.

This definition also leads us into three questions that form the basis of strategic planning:

1   *Where are we now?*
2   *Where do we want to go?*
3   *How do we get there?*

In essence, strategic planning is simply about answering these questions in turn – plus a fourth, which we will introduce in the next chapter.

In the first part of this chapter we explored the term 'strategic planning' and some of its close relatives and considered the different perspectives and types of thinking involved in strategy and planning and the need to engage both – one of the challenges in a strategic planning process. We started to unpick this apparent complexity by considering that there are three dimensions to strategic planning – the context, the process and the content – and shifted the emphasis from a final resulting document to the process. Our working definition emphasised the process, and we have now distilled the aims of that process into three very simple questions that need to be answered.

Compare the statements:

We have to produce a strategic plan.
We are going to work out where we want to go and how we get there.

Whereas the former could appear to be an onerous, daunting and complex task with uncertain implications, the latter conveys that an important but exciting and engaging journey of discovery is about to start – a Strategy Journey.

3

THE HEART OF STRATEGIC PLANNING

In chapter 2 we demystified strategic planning, drilling down to get to a practical working definition and the three core questions that a strategic planning process needs to answer. In this chapter we will look to find what's at the heart of strategic planning.

But first, a confession: in the very early stages of my career, as a young assistant brand manager working at United Biscuits, I was asked to produce a marketing plan for one of the products in the range. I had only a vague notion of what such a plan should contain and absolutely no idea how to begin. (In the years before the world wide web and search engines, sources of knowledge and advice were not as immediately accessible as now.) My levels of worry increased as I struggled to try and work out what I needed to do, anxious to get it right but without the knowledge or experience to make a confident attempt. Fortunately I was rescued by my marketing manager, who guided me through what was required and how to go about developing this and who supported me as I learnt (an example of the excellent coaching and development culture in that organisation at that time; I suspect this was the hidden purpose of the challenge!).

Those facing the challenge of developing a strategic plan for the first time might experience similar concerns and uncertainty: what's required, how do I go about it, where do I start? Unlike my marketing plan learning experience, this will be 'for real' and not a personal development exercise, with significant implications for the organisation and huge risks if it is not undertaken effectively.

These days, buoyed by years of learning and experience, my approach when faced with a major challenge is to use a 'first principles' approach, to work it back to key elements that I can understand and then think through how to tackle it. We will continue this approach to work through how to go about developing a strategic plan.

The four stages (and a circle)

As we saw in chapter 1, some approaches to strategic planning give the impression of a dry, analytical and mechanistic process that is undertaken step by step until the specified content is completed, with daunting tasks to be tackled at each stage. It is easy to see how responsibility for strategic planning was often vested in a small group of corporate planning experts or external management consultants employing an array of sophisticated tools and techniques, such as Boston Consulting Group matrices, value chain analysis, Porter's five forces analysis, scenario planning, net present value evaluation of options, and so on. Credibility appeared to reside in the ability to use these, rather than in determining what the questions are that need answering and then finding the most appropriate way to address these.

Applying a 'first principles' approach, we have restated the challenge of developing a strategic plan as answering three simple questions:

1   *Where are we now?*
2   *Where do we want to go?*
3   *How do we get there?*

This doesn't mean that there is no place for any of the aforementioned strategic analysis techniques; instead it places the emphasis on having to think through how to address these questions, what aspects might be relevant and which techniques could be useful in developing the answers.

So strategic planning can be seen as a process of asking and answering those three questions in turn, and we shall explore later what is involved in this. However, there is also a further, very important challenge that follows the development of an organisation's strategic plan: making it happen. Indeed, this is critically important – a plan without action is irrelevant. Yet despite this, in too many cases less organisational attention and energy are devoted to implementation than to the development of the strategic plan; it seems almost as though there is a collective sense of relief at completing the strategic planning process – job done! – and the organisation returns its attention to getting on with business as usual, and people catch up with the work they have put to one side whilst engaged in the strategic planning 'project'.

This is another very compelling reason not to focus on the strategic plan document as the end result of the process. Instead it should be considered an interim outcome, a stepping stone or platform to galvanise the organisation's next actions and development. Implementing a strategic plan requires just as much collective determination and effort as is expended in its development; although it might not be seen as stimulating an intellectual challenge as developing strategy, arguably it is at least as difficult and equally important (the right strategy not carried out cannot be an effective strategy).

Our three simple but powerful questions form the basis of *developing* a strategic plan. They represent the stages that an organisation needs to work through in this process. However, as we have seen, successful implementation of this plan is a critical part of strategic planning. To make sure that this is not overlooked or merely an afterthought, this is the fourth key stage in our overall strategic planning process. Indeed, an effective strategic plan will have considered how to manage implementation successfully as an integral part of its development.

Table 3.1 Answering the question

Stage	Answering the question	What we need to do
I	Where are we now?	Assess the situation
II	Where do we want to go?	Develop the strategy
III	How do we get there?	Plan and organise
IV	How do we make it happen?	Implement the strategic plan

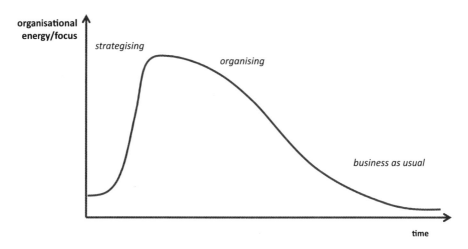

Figure 3.1 Organisational energy

There is another concept about strategic planning that I want to introduce here. In our discourse so far we have presumed that we are considering the usual interpretation of strategic planning as a clearly defined project carried out by the organisation over a particular period of time, an important high-profile exercise that will be repeated at two- or three-year intervals (sometimes more or less frequently). Typically this involves an announced beginning, the assigning of responsibilities and resources, an intensive focused effort and a defined completion process (for example, approval of the completed strategic plan document by the board or an external regulator). The energy levels and focus of the organisation increase and then dissipate as attention switches to implementing the plan and getting on with business as usual.

As this implementation stage progresses – whether successfully or otherwise – inevitably there will be implicit or explicit assessment of how well the strategic plan is being executed and whether it is effective. There will be lessons learnt and observations made about how reality differs from some of the assumptions and forecasts made in developing the plan. New developments that were unforeseen – external or internal – will occur in time, and the possible implications of these will need to be considered. Or maybe the impetus of the strategic plan gradually becomes assimilated into a new established way of operating until there is a desire to re-energise the organisation by looking afresh at its future development. Whichever scenario, and whether or not this is part of a formal process, the situation is being continually assessed. These are in essence examples of starting to ask again, 'Where are we now?' albeit perhaps addressing a particular aspect or circumstance rather than the whole organisation. At some point this might build into a consensus that there have been sufficient significant changes to what was envisaged in the strategic plan to warrant a more collective and coordinated review – the context has changed, prompting the start of a new structured process to modify or renew the strategic plan.

So, returning to our four stages, we can see that these can be considered a cycle, where the need or intent to adapt, revise or renew the organisation's strategic plan arises during or following implementation of the current plan.

Figure 3.2 The four stages

From this perspective we are starting to consider strategic planning as an ongoing process, as a way of continually thinking about the organisation and what its future might be. Whilst there might be periods of intense coordinated organisation-wide focus to concentrate attention and develop an agreed-upon way forward – 'developing the strategic plan' – the key questions are just as pertinent at any time, if only to revalidate the continuing relevance of the current strategic plan.

Strategic planning: the principal activities

As I mentioned earlier in this chapter, strategic planning is often perceived as a complex and difficult challenge that requires the confident application of a formidable array of seemingly sophisticated tools and techniques – and hence is outside the comfort zone of all but a select few. 'Strategy' is exciting but complex – many might want to influence its development but would be apprehensive about taking responsibility for the process. 'Planning' also has its challenges, for example developing projections of future finances and resources. They require different mindsets and skills, yet in strategic planning both are needed, working together seamlessly through the process.

There is an alternative way of considering the principal activities involved in strategic planning and, therefore, what skills are required. Using the terms 'strategising' and 'organising' helps distinguish clearly between these aspects of developing a strategic plan. Strategising is about analysis and turning this into insight; considering possibilities and their implications (scenarios); weighing up options and making decisions. Organising involves planning, assigning and aligning resources, motivating, doing, monitoring and reviewing.

Considering strategising and organising as distinct elements has several advantages. It recognises that there are different types of thinking and processes involved (and hence abilities required). Importantly, it reinforces that an organisation can be continually involved in each. We have seen that strategies often emerge and develop and that organisational priorities and resources change in the light of developments – they are not confined to a formally defined 'strategic planning' project every three or so years; strategising and organising are dynamic activities in which people can engage at any time.

23

Figure 3.3 Strategising and organising

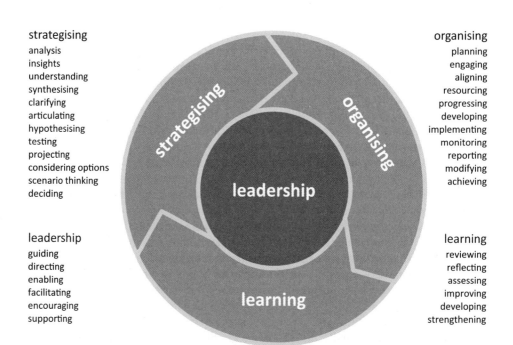

Figure 3.4 Strategic planning: the principal activities

There is another important activity required in effective strategic planning. The skill of *leadership* is to understand how best to stimulate these activities and guide the process, helping create an environment in the organisation to enable these to flourish at the appropriate time. The role of leadership is also to facilitate the discussions, debates and decisions that need to happen in strategising and organising and to coordinate all these various activities and communicate effectively throughout the organisation and with stakeholders about process, progress and outputs. Leadership is a skill that is not confined to seniority in the organisational hierarchy, and responsibility is not vested in a single individual – it can be demonstrated by anyone.

Thinking in this way – about strategising, organising and leadership – helps embed strategic planning at the core of an organisation and engaging people at the heart of it. For me, this is a much healthier view – more dynamic, meaningful and realistic – than the old, dry stereotypical image of strategic planning as a formal distinct exercise additional to 'business as usual', and it is an approach that can help organisations address their futures more successfully.

But there is also a fourth activity that is just as powerful yet often overlooked. *Learning* – both individual and organisational – is an important and underrated dynamic in a strategic planning process. Learning applies in two of the strategic planning 'dimensions'; as analysis and insights help shape the thinking behind the *content* of the plan they can help people see situations in new ways, appreciating the context and understanding the arguments being developed through the strategising. But also people are learning about the *process* of strategic planning, how tools and techniques can be used and adapted to provide clarity, how the process is organised and shaped. Such learning strengthens the strategic planning capabilities of the organisation, giving people more confidence to undertake this in future.

One particular example sticks in my memory. At the end of a particularly intensive but successful strategic planning process with which I had been helping an organisation, buoyed by the positive comments of the board, they asked if I would work with them again when they developed their next strategic plan (in a regulated industry this was a defined annual requirement). It had been a stimulating and enjoyable process, and we had worked well together. It had been that organisation's first experience of strategic planning, and the learning curve had been very steep, but it was apparent to me that one of the benefits (as well as their strategic plan) had been that they now had the ability to tackle the following year's process themselves. (I was happy to work with them again if required, but they would manage without additional help if they chose to do this.)

These four activities – strategising, organising, leadership and learning – are the key components in a strategic planning process, and an organisation needs to have skills and capabilities in each of them, as well as the confidence to apply them.

Making sense

Let us return now to the questions that our four stages are designed to answer:

1   *Where are we now?*
2   *Where do we want to go?*
3   *How do we get there?*
4   *How do we make it happen?*

These are the fundamental and most powerful questions in strategic planning. There is one common word in those four questions: 'we'. It signifies a collective venture towards a common purpose, sharing ownership and responsibility. And the purpose is inquisitive, with an open remit, a quest to articulate clear answers on behalf of the organisation. By taking part in that quest – to whatever extent – people are contributing to determining the organisation's future.

There is a compelling individual as well as organisational motivation to answer these questions. People want to understand their situation, to make sense of where they are and what might happen. Finding meaning and identity is a powerful driver, and the organisation in which they work is a significant social construct whose future affects theirs – they have a vested interest in trying to understand what this might be. At one level this relates to their role in the organisation; at times when there is uncertainty about whether or how this might change, they will expend considerable energy – mental and social – trying to clarify this. Such a dynamic occurs at the team or group level, too, and also on an organisation-wide scale – when something might change, there is a basic need to try and work out what this might be and its implications at all these levels. We all want to make sense of our situation, to understand where we are and what the future might hold.

Strategic planning can be construed as a way in which this can happen for the organisation. The questions posed in our four stages are a logical sequence through which a rationale can be developed to explain organisational choices made and actions taken or planned and to make sense of the organisation's current situation and intended future.

The quest for understanding and meaning is a powerful driver. 'Sensemaking' describes the process by which we engage with others to find a rationale we can understand. We will seek out information that helps us understand our situation and how it might change. We look for cues and signals in conversations with other people, in what we see and what we hear. Actions and behaviours provide clues (frequently prompting adjustment to our thinking). It has to be plausible – we will construct a rationale and then revise or reject it if we discover some inconsistency or something that doesn't make sense, and we continually refine the story that is developing in our minds until we are satisfied we understand it and it has a rational consistency and credibility. Such a process is continual and often subtle and implicit – it's so obvious and natural that we take it for granted and might not recognise that this is what we are doing until it is pointed out to us. Sensemaking has been the subject of a lot of research in recent years, such is its importance as a motivation in the social discourse within organisations and hence how they actually function.

Sensemaking is also a powerful concept to consider in the context of strategic planning. Fundamentally, the aim of strategic planning is to enable the organisation to make sense of its situation and decide how it wants to develop in the future – as expressed in the questions; our four stages provide an outline framework to answer these. So one view of strategic planning is to consider it a means to facilitate sensemaking in an organisation.

But the concept of sensemaking also gives us a different way of thinking about how we go about strategic planning and what is important in the process. Sensemaking occurs by people talking, listening, reading, observing and considering – a continual but transient process whereby once something has appeared to make sense people move on to the implications of this or to new topics, revisiting their understanding only if they encounter something that is inconsistent or otherwise creates doubt. So the basic aim in a strategic planning process is to facilitate this sensemaking, to provide opportunities for people to think through our fundamental questions and collectively come up with answers.

Although this sounds simple, there is still a major challenge involved in coming up with answers. Sensemaking is an iterative process, forming initial constructs and then modifying or rejecting these in the light of new information or others' views. The nature of sensemaking is to satisfy the need for understanding with plausible solutions, but without robust challenge and testing plausibility could be accepted at the expense of accuracy – so questioning and challenge are a vital part of the process of organisational sensemaking in a strategic planning process.

So in this way of looking at strategic planning, what we are doing is providing a framework within which organisational sensemaking can happen. We are enabling and facilitating the exchange of information, the sharing of views, the conversations and debate through which we will develop answers to our questions. Our model of four stages provides an outline structure, and we can help within each stage by framing more detailed questions to focus attention and stimulate thinking. We also need to provide the opportunities for this discourse, the time and space for people to engage in thinking and talking; we are facilitating conversations.

But not just any conversations. These conversations need to be of a depth and quality that enables ideas to be shared and interpretations clarified, to encourage questioning and challenge, to explore implications and alternatives. They need to be allowed and encouraged to proceed until meanings are understood and understanding is tested. Such 'rich conversations' are different to most of the verbal interchanges that occur in organisations. These tend to be transactional, giving or seeking information, instructing or reporting on action, rather than exploring interpretation and meaning to any depth. Rich conversations allow assumed views to be challenged and new information to be assimilated and have the intention of achieving understanding of one's own and others' thinking and the openness to changing either of these.

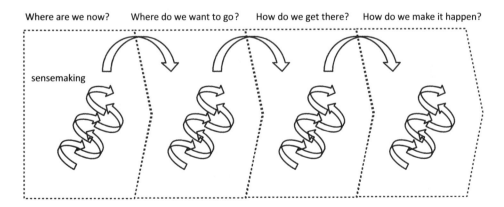

Figure 3.5 Strategic planning as sensemaking

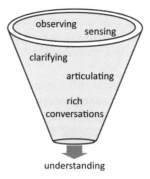

Figure 3.6 Rich conversations

Considered in this way, a strategic planning process is all about finding ways for such rich conversations to occur, developing shared meaning through an organisational journey to construct a cohesive response to the challenge of the four questions.

This defines the leadership challenge at the core of strategic planning. Our four questions provide an outline framework for the stages of the journey. But within each there needs to be a more detailed plan of how to go about this, to bring together effectively the information, analysis, insights, perspectives, theories, decision-making and communications needed – and the skill to adapt that plan as the process develops. What are the key aspects to consider, who should be involved, what is the most appropriate format to enable this to be considered, how can this be discussed effectively, what happens next? All these questions are part of the thinking that needs to occur to guide the process.

Creating the right conditions in which such 'rich conversations' can develop is important, but often not easy; in the busy-ness of working it can be difficult to carve out suitable times when those people who ought to be involved or who could contribute can come together. It takes time also for people to tune in their thinking, both to the question being considered and for the discussions to develop to a level where meaning is being explored and tested. An environment and atmosphere which encourage this contribute too; space for thinking has both physical and temporal aspects. Setting up the discussion with the right stimuli, providing clarity of context and questions and encouraging a mindset conducive to collective deliberation with due focus, commitment and energy are all part of the craft of guiding the process, as is how to continue the conversations especially when other tasks will intervene and interrupt the thinking.

Rich conversations are not confined to planned opportunities, of course – sometimes clarity of meaning can occur through a one-sentence exchange. Nor does sensemaking occur only through such conversations. It is rather an ongoing, often implicit quest for understanding that uses every piece of relevant information to check and refine current meanings. Cues occur in actions and behaviours as much as spoken or written words, and the political dynamics of organisational hierarchies and social position can influence the weight attached to these. A good example of the impact of this is in how people assess the culture of their organisation; they are making sense of the unwritten rules of how the organisation works from a myriad of cues, notably the dynamics of power and influence and the behaviours they see around them.

Facilitating understanding

We have explored in this chapter the four stages and fundamental questions that provide a framework for a strategic planning process and the activities of strategising, organising, learning and leadership that are involved. The concept of sensemaking – and the contribution of rich conversations to this – is a powerful way of considering the nature of individual and collective thinking and the development of meaning that needs to occur in strategic planning; and a strategic planning process can be seen as a journey by which an organisation makes sense of its own situation and comes to decide its desired future.

This desire to make sense of what it's about; where it fits in its market, industry, community and society; what its purpose is; and what it's aiming to achieve, and how, is a powerful driver at the core of every organisation, whether commercial, non-profit, public, academic, healthcare or social. It is a basic common need for people to try to understand where they fit in their organisation, what its purpose is and how their contribution helps.

Strategic planning provides a framework in which this thinking and development can take place. It is the process by which the organisation attempts to answer these questions. Importantly, this may or may not be a conscious, formal, structured activity; it may or may not occur within a defined time frame; there may or may not be any written document; it may or may not answer all the questions at the same time. In spirit, strategic planning is a living activity. How this thinking occurs in an organisation, how directions and intentions are decided, how people come to understand what they can contribute – all are more part of the culture of the organisation than they are any documented formal procedure. Strategic planning is about hearts as well as minds – it is about the people in an organisation and their understanding, motivation and contribution. It is really all about identifying opportunities, setting directions, aligning the organisation and making it happen – through whatever processes are right for that organisation.

For strategic planning is about people. It's the activity, the framework, the process by which they gain a common understanding of their organisation. It's about creating a shared language, shared pictures, impressions and stories that enable them to make sense of what they are doing and defining where the organisation should be heading and how it should develop. It's about what people can focus on and do to make a difference, how they can contribute.

With this philosophy in mind we can refine our earlier working definition to reflect this fundamental motivation:

> *Strategic planning is how the people in an organisation make sense of where it's going and how it's going to get there.*

Strategic planning is about people engaged in a common purpose to understand and articulate how they want their organisation to move forward. The term 'strategy journey' seems to me to convey the exploration and adventure involved – and it captures how an organisation thinks, decides, communicates and adapts as it works out where it wants to go and how it's going to get there.

It also reflects the nature of how strategies and plans develop. In a continually changing environment it's the ability of an organisation to adapt and evolve that is key; a strategic plan just crystallises the organisation's thinking and intentions at a particular time. Its real value is as a platform, a guide and a stimulus to action and to shape how the organisation makes decisions and modifies its behaviours as the future unfolds.

Strategic planning – whatever we might choose to call it – is about depth and meaning within an organisation. Although the context for each organisation, the process by which it is developed and the style and detail of its content will vary, it is the way in which the organisation makes sense of its purpose, how it meets its customers' needs, how people work together to make this happen. It is about developing understanding – thinking and communication – and inspiring people to commit their knowledge, skills and energies towards a common goal. This – involving the minds and the hearts of the people in the organisation – is what ultimately makes strategic planning so powerful, alive and relevant. It's people that are at the heart of strategic planning.

Part II

HOW TO DEVELOP A STRATEGIC PLAN

4

WHY DEVELOP A STRATEGIC PLAN?

In part 1 of this book we looked at some of the ways in which strategic planning has developed and examined the various schools of thought. We then sought to adopt a first principles approach to help demystify the perceptions of complexity and sophistication that have grown up around strategic planning, drawing a distinction between the context, the process and the content 'dimensions', and we identified the four fundamental questions to be addressed in developing a strategic plan and so provide an outline framework of the stages involved to answer these. We considered the principal activities – strategising, organising, learning and leadership – and introduced the concept of sensemaking as a powerful motivation and how it could be considered as an organisational dynamic at the core of the strategic planning process. We have demystified strategic planning into a process focused on enabling people in an organisation to make sense of where it is going and to work out how it is going to get there.

Part 2 looks at how to go about developing a strategic plan – how to consider the context, the process and the content and some of the factors and approaches that influence these. It is intended as a practical guide, not to specific analytical tools or techniques and how they are used, but to help the reader think through what approach might be appropriate for his or her organisation at a particular time. Rather than attempt to provide a comprehensive handbook of all the scenarios, approaches and techniques that could be applicable (there are already excellent books covering these), I will make liberal use of examples to try and illustrate some of these and what might influence when and how they might be used. I hope this will help to bring such choices to life in a way that helps the reader consider what might be appropriate for their own organisation.

We will start by looking at the context and reasons to develop a strategic plan and how these influence the ensuing strategy journey.

The need for a strategic plan

What prompts an organisation to develop a strategic plan? Every organisation's circumstances and rationale will be different. However, it might be helpful to consider two questions: a) what has prompted the decision to embark on that particular strategy journey, and b) what is determining the principal approach that is driving this?

To illustrate this, let's look at four scenarios:

A   Company A operates in a regulated industry. The regulatory body requires all companies to submit a strategic plan that meets defined criteria by a specified deadline.

One example of this occurred in the UK financial services industry in the early 2000s, when the regulator at the time, the Financial Services Authority, required all providers of financial services to produce strategic plans that included financial projections with scenarios for varying economic and market conditions. This prompted a rush of strategic planning activity with consequent stretching of resources amongst those organisations who had been accustomed to reporting on narrower financial viability criteria to the previous regulator.

A more recent example was in 2014, when Monitor, the regulatory body for NHS Foundation Trusts, introduced compulsory five-year strategic planning including issuing best practice guidelines and minimum requirement frameworks. One purpose for this was to be able to collate an overview of the NHS Foundation Trusts hospital sector at a time of severe NHS funding challenges and assess the hospitals' capabilities and vulnerabilities within the sector. (I will return in a later chapter to the factors that made this a somewhat futile exercise strategically.)

B   The new board of Corporation B decides they need to undertake a review of their operating divisions and assess how each will fit strategically and contribute to the corporation's ambitions; they also want to test the capabilities of their divisions' senior executive teams. A small head office team is set up to drive forward and coordinate the strategic planning process across the divisions, setting out the process with specific requirements, timelines and formats for the resulting outputs. (Of course, much energy is expended here as the divisional teams compete with each other to achieve all the milestones and demonstrate their abilities with sophisticated charts, glossy presentations and comprehensive appendices!)

C   After several years of steady sales growth supported by investment in marketing and manufacturing equipment to improve productivity and capacity, the future is looking less certain for Company C. One of their competitors has just been acquired by a US group with a reputation for stripping out costs and low-cost production techniques, and people across Company C are beginning to worry about what might happen. The marketers are concerned about the consequences of a high-volume/low-price drive from their competitor for market share, the financial director is anxious about the impact on margins, and the production team fears the consequence will ultimately be the transfer of manufacturing to low-cost factories in China. Meanwhile, sales managers are talking up the risk of salespeople leaving to join the competitor as it builds its sales force, although HR think this is just a ruse to increase sales force remuneration. As the various concerns are raised more frequently and volubly it becomes apparent to all that there needs to be a more structured process to consider all the implications and decide on how Company C should respond.

D   Entrepreneurial technology start-up D has evolved over five years to a medium-sized organisation spread over several sites. As the organisation has grown some supporting infrastructure has been introduced, but working practices and bonus arrangements vary considerably across the different locations, and there are differing approaches to outsourcing or in-company resourcing of supporting technical and non-core services. Department heads have tabled several opportunities for future development of their product areas, ranging from acquisition of new technologies to scaling up manufacturing. Whilst people are still keen to promote their own views, a consensus gradually forms that D needs a collective process to consider all these issues and opportunities and decide on the next phase of its development.

Considering these examples from the perspective of the two questions posed earlier, in the case of both Company A and Company C it is *external* factors (the industry regulator and a threat from a competitor respectively) that have prompted their decisions to develop their strategic plans; whereas Corporation B and technology start-up D were driven by *internal* situations (a formal review of the future direction in the case of B and the need for a clear, cohesive and understood strategy across the organisation for D).

The principal approaches that are driving the process also differ in these examples: A and B are adopting a *deliberate* approach to formulating their strategic plans, setting out clear parameters and a structured process; whereas in the cases of C and D their strategy journeys have *emerged* from a growing realisation that there was a need to find a collective way to address various issues.

One important point to note is that these are the factors that are relevant for each of those organisations at that particular time; they might not be the reasons why the organisations develop future strategic plans. Let's consider what might transpire for each of them:

A   Future strategic planning at regulated Company A is likely to continue to be strongly influenced – and perhaps determined – by what the regulator requires. This might specify a strategic plan and supporting information in a defined format (enabling the regulator to compile a sector or industry overview) and include steps in the process such as comprehensive risk assessments or stress testing the company financial plans in stated scenarios. Company A will become adept at

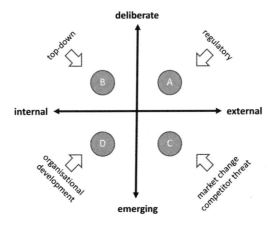

Figure 4.1 Why develop a strategic plan?

responding to these requirements and will build this into its annual planning process. Radical transformational initiatives such as acquisitions and divestments might be dealt with outside this process by separate regulatory procedures: the scope of the formal strategic plan becomes narrowed to meet the regulator's needs rather than encompass Company A's wider strategic canvas (so, for example, topics such as company values, brand positioning and people strategies might not form part of this). However, developing strategies and plans for these areas will still happen, but perhaps in separate processes.

A dual-level approach to strategy development and strategic planning is not uncommon. An example of this is when there are highly sensitive and confidential options being explored, such as a merger, acquisition or disposal: the strategic planning process might already be underway based on the known current situation, and this is allowed to proceed given the uncertainty and necessary secrecy about these options. Another example is when there are hidden political motives: the ulterior purpose of developing the strategic plan document is to impress external regulators or corporation-level management whilst decisions continue to be taken irrespective of this work.

In the case of Company A, arguably the strategic planning process is as much focused at the industry level as the organisation level. The regulator has the opportunity to consider how a sector might develop in future and what initiatives and changes are required to enable this to happen. However, unless this is explicitly understood (and an objective) there is a risk that the mechanics of collating the strategic plans prepared by Company A and its competitors result merely in a summary 'health check' of the state of the sector, without the strategic planning process necessary to decide and articulate a convincing view of the future.

Strategic planning in a regulated industry need not be so constrained in scope, however. The regulator's strategy might be to ensure those organisations operating in a particular sector are robustly independently sustainable and competitive, and the aim is to encourage innovation to stimulate market change or drive industry reconfiguration through consolidation of the players in the sector. As always, it all depends . . . !

B   Corporation B is another example where it is important to be clear about the level at which the strategic planning process is aimed. Whilst the divisions are developing their individual strategic plans, the rationale is to inform a strategic assessment at corporation level of 'where are we now, and what might be the options and factors influencing future development?' So this is the first stage in a corporation-level strategic planning process; whilst the strategic plans developed by the constituent divisions might also be valuable within these organisations, their scope and ability to implement these are determined by the nature of their relationship to the corporation. There is likely to be more opportunity for self-determination in a group of semi-autonomous companies operating in different industry or market sectors than in a corporation tightly structured with market sector or geographically focused divisions.

However, much depends also on how the strategic planning process is designed. Suppose that the divisions are fully involved in the development of the corporation's strategic plan, rather than just providing high-quality informa- tion as inputs to the strategic assessment stage; they will develop their stra- tegic plans in a clearly articulated context and will be major players in the strategy journey upon which the corporation is embarking to decide how it wants to develop.

C   Unlike our previous two examples, manufacturing company C has a high degree of autonomy (although its shareholders could be a major consideration in any decisions that affect financial expectations). However, at the stage we have described in the scenario the key need is for the organisation to make sense of several changes, potential changes and challenges – external and internal – that might affect its future.

The challenge here is to find a way of enabling these pressing factors to be considered within a structured strategic planning process. As well as external developments that appear to be threats, there are valid concerns from internal stakeholders, each of whom is championing a particular agenda to press for resolution of their current issue. They will need to have confidence in the process and be reas- sured about their opportunities to participate and that it will lead to answers.

These issues help define the context and hence the scope of the strategic planning process. Too broad and their concerns might receive too little attention; too deep and fundamental and the issues will be subsumed; too comprehensive and the answers they need will take too long. Yet the thinking needs to be thorough and sufficiently framed so other important factors aren't missed or excluded.

The strategic planning process will be judged on how successfully people in the organisation work together on this and how effectively it deals with the issues currently causing concern (for example initiatives to reduce the potential impact of the threat). How the organisation approaches strategic planning in the future will be influenced by this experience (and perceptions about it). There needs to be a lot of thought and discussion given to working out what process is appropriate and explaining this carefully; given the internal context there might need to be some work undertaken on organisational relationships.

D   Technology company D has undergone rapid growth – internally and externally – and there's a lot of energy in the organisation to continue this. However, people recognise that the challenge is how to channel this energy. There is clear accept- ance that the organisation needs to clarify its thinking through developing a stra- tegic plan to determine the next phase of its development, and it seems likely that people will be keen to do this – for example, they want to make sense of where they should focus their efforts in new product development, which sectors and markets give the best opportunities for sales growth, what investments to make in manufacturing, which areas to outsource and how to create consistent company- wide rewards structures and policies.

The challenge here in working out a strategic planning process is how to organise such enthusiasm. People will be keen to get started. They are likely to become impatient or disillusioned if the process is too slow or cumbersome, yet there is a risk of disconnected thinking or too narrow a picture if the work on the various topics is not scoped at the right levels and proceeds at different paces.

One approach would be to begin the process by organising work on each of the areas to develop assessments of the current situation as inputs to start the collective discussions about the organisation's current position and how it might develop. These will help define the agenda for the process that ensues, although there might be other aspects for consideration as this develops. A few key themes of work might emerge, and the resulting strategic plan might focus just on these rather than encompassing every aspect and function of the organisation – in effect, its less comprehensive approach might be a strength rather than a weakness.

These examples illustrate the importance of understanding the context *before* working out what strategic planning process might be appropriate, and they demonstrate some of the range of approaches that might be taken. They also show that there is no 'best practice' method of going about this, involving a series of techniques such as market analysis, SWOT (Strengths, Weaknesses, Opportunities and Threats), board workshop and so on, leading to the production of a document containing all the detailed plans. It is what's right for the organisation that matters, not ticking the boxes in textbooks.

The context for each organisation at a particular time is unique, and an effective strategic planning process will recognise this. Consider the analogy of planning an important journey. You need to consider who is in your party, what their preferences are and any limitations they might have. What will terrain be like, and what might be the best mode of transport for each stage of the journey? Does the nature of the journey require a lot of equipment and provisions to be carried, or is it preferable to travel light and pick up what's required on the way? What preparation is required beforehand, and is some of this delegated to individual members of the party? What roles and influence might they want in either planning the journey or when it has started, and what is the best way to keep the party travelling well together? If injuries or obstacles slow progress, how might these be dealt with? And so on . . .

Just as all these considerations occur when planning a physical journey, so there is much to think about in preparing for an organisation's strategy journey. The journey analogy is a helpful way of approaching strategic planning. It reinforces that this is about people, where they want to get to, how they interact, what they experience together, what they discover along the way. Journeys take people to a different place; strategic planning does the same for organisations.

Time and energy

The concept of strategic planning as an organisation's strategy journey is useful also when we consider the lifecycle of a strategic plan. The phase of developing a strategic plan is usually one of intense organisational focus and effort, carried forward with determination into the implementation phase. As touched on in chapter 3, this momentum dissipates in time as initiatives are progressed (or not, in some cases), changes become assimilated into 'business as usual' activity and new issues and opportunities arise that take up the attention of the organisation.

It can be helpful to consider as part of the context for an organisation where it sits on this lifecycle curve (whether or not there has been an earlier strategic planning process; similar patterns can be seen in organisations that have undergone significant changes or periods of rapid development). The need and the appetite for strategic planning

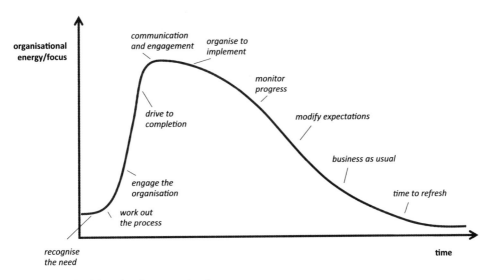

Figure 4.2 The lifecycle of a strategic plan

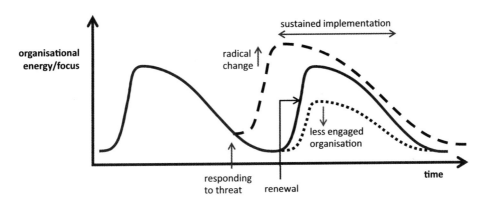

Figure 4.3 Refreshing the strategic plan

can depend on this; the strategic leadership skill is in assessing these. Embarking on a strategic planning process is a major commitment of organisational resources – people, energy and focus – with potentially significant negative impact should it fail or falter.

Deciding when is the right time to commit to a strategy journey requires good judgement – one of the attributes of strategic leadership. As we have seen in the illustrative examples in this chapter, the need and motivation for this can arise in different ways. Radical changes (external or internal) can prompt the need to reconsider the organisation's current strategic plan, or it might be the case that the impetus of the current strategic plan has been lost, and the organisation would benefit from a reinvigoration of focus and energy through a renewal of the strategic plan.

In the case of organisations like Company A, where in a couple of years the main reason for undertaking a strategic planning process might be because it has become an established part of a regular planning cycle (whether internally or externally determined), if there have been no significant changes in the context for the organisation the process might focus on refreshing the plan and its implementation rather than reviewing the organisation's strategy.

Changing contexts

Let us consider how the strategy journeys might map out for one organisation over the course of a few years, as illustrated in Figure 4.4.

The organisation's first strategic plan set a clear direction, and in the initial stages of implementation this intended strategy was being realised. But progress started to drift from this – initiatives faltered, new products didn't achieve the projected sales, assumptions used in financial planning turned out to be too optimistic given changes in the market, competitors increased their market share more than expected, technological innovations changed customers' requirements: any of the many ways that real life can turn out differently from what was anticipated.

Although there was increasing deviation from the original strategic plan, there was still sufficient recognition that the basic strategic direction remained relevant as a broad goal, even if the organisation had fallen somewhat behind its intended plan to implement this. The ambition still resonated with people in the organisation, and a rationale had been accepted by the board for why the actual, realised strategic plan differed from the intended – even if some suspected there were initiatives which hadn't been implemented as well as they should have been.

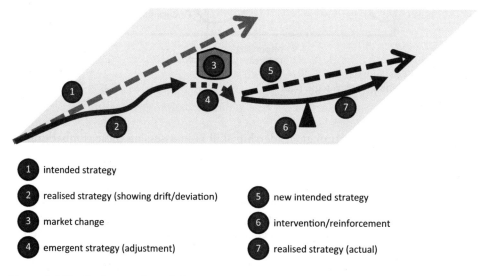

1 intended strategy

2 realised strategy (showing drift/deviation)

3 market change

4 emergent strategy (adjustment)

5 new intended strategy

6 intervention/reinforcement

7 realised strategy (actual)

Figure 4.4 Realised versus intended strategy

Towards the end of the second year of the strategic plan one of the organisation's competitors introduced a technological breakthrough that would change the market; it was apparent to all that this would undermine sales of several of the organisation's leading products. After initially trying to throw doubts on the efficacy of the innovation, when it became clear that consumers were switching to this new technology the organisation reacted by exploring options to enable it to compete, including potential acquisition of manufacturers with the capability to replicate the innovation to stepping up its own research and development programme to find a patentable alternative. The efforts to respond to the new threat resulted in the organisation acquiring a different technology that offered other product benefits, and a strategy began to emerge about how this could be developed, including entry into new market segments.

The implications of this for the organisation needed to be considered, and a strategic plan was developed to work out what changes were needed to be able to support this new direction, including disinvesting in some activities and changing the structure of the organisation. However, several assumptions were made in the new intended strategic plan that turned out to be wide of the mark (understandable in a fast-changing market at the early stages of adopting new technologies, but not without some internal retributions), and within the first year it was apparent that the financial plan would not be achieved. A series of crisis discussions was convened, resulting in reducing operational overheads by closing down the manufacture of some less profitable products, and gradually financial performance improved and the organisation was able to begin to pull back towards its intended strategic plan.

This fictional example illustrates some of the strategy journeys that one organisation could experience over the course of a few years, including how events can make strategic plans no longer relevant and the way in which strategies can emerge without a formal strategic planning process – and sometimes need to be developed rapidly in response to significant changes.

One very useful way of looking at this is to consider this as a series of changing contexts. There was one context when the organisation started its first strategic planning process; then there was a different context as a gap developed between this and what was happening. The market-changing competitor innovation was a significant new context that prompted the need to respond, although not by instigating a formal organisation-wide strategic planning process. At each stage there was a new context, and the organisation had to judge how best to address the four key questions, assessing its current situation, considering its options and making decisions about where it wanted to go and then organising to do this and making this happen.

This concept of assessing the context and deciding when it is appropriate to undertake a strategy journey – and of what type – is a vitally important aspect of the strategic leadership we identified as one of the four principal strategic planning activities.

One of the criticisms often directed at strategic planning is that the pace of change is so fast these days that organisations need to be able to respond rapidly. Strategic plans are so quickly out of date that there is no point investing effort in their development for so little relevance. However, this would seem to be based on the somewhat limiting traditional interpretation of strategic planning as the development of a rigid long-term plan; my view of strategic planning is that it is an

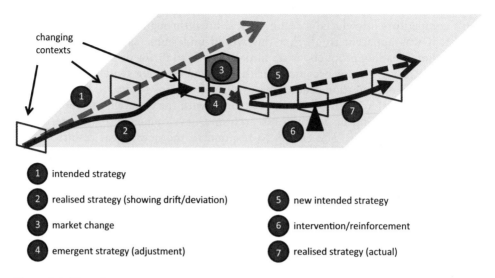

1 intended strategy

2 realised strategy (showing drift/deviation)

3 market change

4 emergent strategy (adjustment)

5 new intended strategy

6 intervention/reinforcement

7 realised strategy (actual)

Figure 4.5 Changing contexts

adaptable, dynamic and ongoing way in which an organisation can decide how to respond to challenges and opportunities and organise to make this happen. Inherent in this is the continual assessment of context and the application of leadership judgement to decide which aspects of the fundamental questions might need to be addressed.

Effective strategic planning gives clarity to the people in the organisation: when they understand where the organisation wants to go and why they are more likely to be able to adapt to changing circumstances, either by revising their plans consistent with the organisation's current strategies or else by realising that they need to revisit these strategies because the context has changed so significantly. Without that investment in understanding, these responses could be inconsistent with the organisation's desired strategic goals.

In this chapter we have looked at what might prompt an organisation to develop a strategic plan and how context is important in determining the nature of the process and the emphasis of the work that ensues, including taking account of the perspectives of people who have a particular interest in what transpires. We have considered the investment of organisational energy in strategic planning and some of the factors that influence when it is the right time to start this, including when to take action to adapt and when to build on what might be emerging. Assessing the need and the context requires astute judgement, and working out how to go about the strategy journey is an important strategic leadership challenge. We have seen how the strategy journeys that an organisation undertakes might differ over time as real life overtakes the assumptions and implementation of even the best strategic plans, and, importantly, we have expounded the idea of such strategy journeys being the organisation's dynamic response to changing contexts.

5

THE PROCESS

In the previous chapter we showed how the strategic planning process is shaped by context, both external and internal, and explored some examples to illustrate what this process might be in various contexts. We have put forward the concept of strategic planning as an organisation's strategy journey, enabling the people in the organisation to make sense of its current situation and decide how it should develop. Such strategy journeys are based on addressing four fundamental questions:

1   *Where are we now?*
2   *Where do we want to go?*
3   *How do we get there?*
4   *How do we make it happen?*

As such, they involve the principal activities of strategising, organising, learning and leadership; the challenge in strategic planning is to orchestrate the process to enable the effective collective application of these. Importantly, we have advocated the idea that this concept of strategy journeys can be applied to a broad spectrum of contexts where an organisation seeks to answer these questions through such a process, including those where urgency of response or a more selective focus on key areas results in a strategy journey that differs from the comprehensive organisational-wide strategic plan development that is the traditional perception of strategic planning.

We now turn our attention to how we might go about organising the strategic planning process and navigating the ensuing strategy journey. But first we have to know where we want to get to . . .

Framing the challenge

We discussed the importance of context in chapter 4; here we expand on this more specifically with the aim of showing how it influences the design of the process.

As we saw in the examples used in chapter 4, the reasons for developing a strategic plan can vary considerably, including meeting external requirements or expectations, understanding how different businesses might fit with the organisation's future strategy, needing to address a number of issues and opportunities across the organisation in a cohesive and coordinated way and working out the next stage of the organisation's development. Strategic planning is often used following major organisational changes as a way of people and teams working out what their role is, how they will work together to contribute to the organisation's success and what that should look like. The stimulus to undertake this can occur rapidly, as in the case of top-down internal or external direction, or a steady build-up of issues and challenges could lead to a consensus that a structured approach is needed.

Regardless of the way in which the decision has come about, what is important is to understand the underlying reasons that have prompted it. Three questions can help define what is required:

- *Why undertake this journey?*

    More specifically, 'What is the reason for considering a strategic planning process for this organisation at this particular time?' As we discussed in the previous chapter, strategic planning requires the investment of much organisational energy – physical, mental and emotional – and is not without risk. The outcomes are uncertain; the process might fail to deliver any content of value (issues can remain unresolved, strategies developed without rigour or articulated vaguely, priorities not clarified); and disagreements about future direction can lead to schisms within the organisation. Consequently, whether to undertake such a venture is an important decision.

    There are a wide variety of reasons why organisations might consider developing a strategic plan. Some are to do with the outcomes, whilst in other cases the process itself serves a purpose. Often the reasons are quite clear, but some are more 'under the surface', aimed at improving how the organisation functions. Table 5.1 shows a few examples. It is not intended to be a comprehensive list, but just to illustrate the range of reasons which an organisation might choose to address through strategic planning.

    Often it is a combination of these that prompt the need for a structured process to resolve them and work through the implications within a cohesive framework; sometimes the reasons can be difficult to uncover at first, perhaps contained in a more general feeling that 'things aren't quite right' in a number of areas. Or, as in the case of an externally directed requirement to produce a strategic plan, the consequent rationale from the point of view of the organisation might be to demonstrate competence and financial sustainability.

    It is important to make clear that this refers to what is perceived as a reason to consider developing a strategic plan before the outset; there might be very different outcomes by the time this particular strategy journey has concluded.

Table 5.1 Reasons for developing a strategic plan

Making strategic decisions	Organising resources	Organisation development
Acquisition/disposal	Projects/initiatives	Refocus/restructure
New markets/sectors	IT/systems development	Culture change
Sales channel priorities	Capability/competency gaps	Competence
R&D focus	Longer-term projections	Clarify vision/purpose
Investment priorities	Manufacturing configuration	Focus/motivate/align
Portfolio strategy	Productivity/efficiency	Organisational values
Financial sustainability	Outsourcing	Performance/rewards

- *What are the critical questions we need to answer?*

The next step in considering the strategic planning process is to identify some of the specific questions that it is important to try to answer during the journey. It is perfectly valid of course to develop a strategic plan that considers all aspects of the organisation from first principles, a comprehensive review of everything the organisation does or could possibly do. But even in this case some drawing of boundaries and narrowing of scope needs to occur, during the process if not at the beginning, if the strategy journey is to remain manageable and completed in a reasonable period of time (there are only so many combinations of options the brain can consider).

What we are doing in considering this question is expanding out from the reasons we have identified for undertaking this to think through what we need to include and so help shape the process accordingly. This is perhaps most easily illustrated by an example: we will use the case of the organisation that is required to develop its strategic plan and submit this to the industry regulator. From the organisation's point of view, what it is aiming to do is to demonstrate its financial sustainability and its competence so that it continues to receive regulatory approval to continue to operate in that sector.

The mind-map diagram that follows shows the initial outline thinking about the topic areas that might be relevant in reviewing its financial sustainability and the various aspects of organisational competence (it is not meant to be comprehensive, merely to demonstrate how such thinking might be developed).

As the areas for consideration are mapped, some of the links between them become apparent – in this case, as an example the organisation will want to demonstrate its competency in assessing and managing risk by stress testing its financial projections against several scenarios. So even at this initial stage of thinking about the process we are seeing that one of the themes of work will be to develop projections supported by clear assumptions that can be modelled in some realistic and also stretching scenarios (which will need to be developed).

Figure 5.1 Framing the challenge

This does not of course exclude other significant areas that need to be considered or narrow the scope of the strategic plan. Yet what it does help is in thinking through how some key areas of the work might develop and so aid in starting to consider ideas for how this might be organised.

Identifying critical questions to be answered continues throughout the strategic planning process. It's a crucial part of the journey (in our analogy of a physical journey, a map gives only one level of information about what might be encountered; as one travels along the route there will be choices about the specific path to be taken).

I will draw on an example from my own experience to illustrate this. Progress in this particular strategic planning project was going well following the process that had been mapped out after much thought in the initial stages, but then the thinking on two parallel workstreams converged to a point about priorities that people were struggling to resolve. After a couple of unsuccessful attempts to find a way through this obstacle, the strategic planning leadership team took a step back and looked at the situation using the type of thinking illustrated in the prior example. Once they had identified that at the root of the problem was the allocation of scarce resources (IT systems development in this particular case) they were able to adapt the process to focus on this and quickly negotiate a way to resolve the issue. This was a question that was identified as critical only as the thinking developed in the various streams of work.

- *Who is interested?*

Although it might be tempting to give a flippant answer to a question expressed so simply, its openness is deliberate. In thinking about what type of process would be appropriate we need to consider who we want or need to be involved in this in any way. Which individuals and groups, either within the organisation or external to it, have some interest in the process and its outcomes, and in each case, what is the nature of their interest? What should be their role, involvement and responsibilities – and at which stages of the process are these applicable?

So, for example, in our regulated company illustration, the regulator needs to know that this is happening as they have directed; they might require reassurance that the areas they are interested in are being included and that the process is robust, and an output that meets their requirements needs to be submitted to them by the deadline specified. They might then want to review the contents and clarify various aspects.

Within the organisation there are many interested parties; the challenge is to work out how each of them should be involved. So, for example, what role will the board play – active engagement in all or selected aspects, contributing inputs at key stages, receiving updates and progress reports, making or ratifying decisions, reviewing and formally approving formal outputs (documents or otherwise) or all of these? How are teams, functions and departments going to be involved, and feel involved, without the process becoming cumbersome? How will various groups be consulted, and how might communication be managed to update them? What might need to be dealt with confidentially, and what parts of the work can be shared openly? Will outputs be tailored to meet the interests of different groups?

Again, an example to illustrate: a strategic planning process that is considering potential acquisitions and disposals, or possible outsourcing or other work-force reductions, will need to progress its work with considerable sensitivity and appropriate confidentiality, whereas a strategic plan document for a public service organisation might be published for anyone to read.

The key point here is that it is now, when considering how to design the process, mapping out the various groups and thinking through how and at what stages they should be involved, that we can form an idea of how this might fit into the strategy journey that we are about to plan. In particular, this is useful for the following:

- Mapping out interactions with those groups having formal influence on the strategic plan – e.g., external regulatory bodies to whom documents have to be submitted, such as a board or other governing body that will approve the resulting strategic plan but that has also a steering influence and needs to contribute to its development along the way
- Ensuring that all stakeholders, and others who need to have access to any formal outputs, are considered at the outset of the process rather than risk belated consideration as an afterthought following the intensity of the strategy journey; an analogy in a physical journey is remembering to take with you the contact details of everyone to whom you want to send a postcard (or message from an internet cafe)
- Considering how people across the organisation will know what is going on, what the relationship and communication should be between those directly involved in a particular aspect of the process and their wider departments or functions and also how those areas of the organisation not directly involved at a particular stage are represented or kept informed.

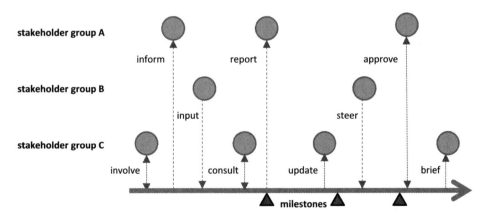

Figure 5.2 Involving stakeholders

By asking these three questions we will now have an understanding of what are the main reasons for undertaking a strategic planning process at this time; what are likely to be some of the critical areas that will need to be considered; and who should be involved and how, and at what stages of the journey on which the organisation is soon to embark. With this as context, we are ready to begin to make plans for the journey.

Planning the journey

Let us recap some of what we've discussed about the strategic planning process.

*   We have said that it's about asking four simple but fundamental questions:

    1   *Where are we now?*
    2   *Where do we want to go?*
    3   *How do we get there?*
    4   *How do we make it happen?*

    . . . and answering these through the principal activities of *strategising*, *organising*, *learning* and *leadership*.
*   The quality of the thinking and communication is paramount; people (and the organisation) are trying to make sense of the organisation's situation and understand its future direction.
*   We can help this by enabling people to engage in 'rich conversations', discussing and challenging information, insights, ideas and opinions, to help develop shared meaning and a common basis for understanding.

So our challenge in planning the strategy journey is to work out how to bring the right people together at the right times with the appropriate information and guidance to facilitate such conversations.

And we know from our earlier thinking who some of the key people are, and how they might need to be involved, as well as some of the important areas that are likely to need to be addressed.

So now we can begin to map out an outline shape to the journey; to refer to the physical analogy, we know the reasons for our journey, a sense of the terrain, who will be involved and in which ways and some of the landmarks or obstacles we shall encounter.

To help our thinking about the process I will break this down into three considerations: *what* gets discussed, *how* it gets discussed and *when*.

The questions beneath the questions

Strategic planning is all about answering questions; the skill lies in asking the right ones. And framing these questions in the right way can help us work out what steps we need to take to answer them.

To illustrate this, we will first look at a fairly typical outline framework for a strategic planning process. Several key focus areas are considered to help form an overall assessment about where the organisation is currently; assumptions are developed about what might change over the next few years, and options are developed for paths

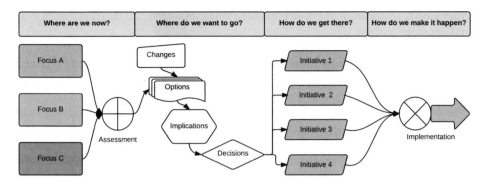

Figure 5.3 Planning the journey

the organisation could follow in light of these. The likely implications and risks of these different strategic options are evaluated to inform decisions about which direction the organisation should take and hence where it wants to go. The next stages are to work out the initiatives and changes to enable this to happen, how to organise resources to implement these and then how to monitor and reinforce or adapt this strategic plan as the journey progresses.

Let us take an example of an organisation that wants to reassess its overall strategy given significant changes that have already or will soon affect it – either in its industry or market or internally. It could be the case that sales of the current range of products that it manufactures are declining in the face of changing consumer preferences and its factories need major investment to match the unit production costs of its main competitor or that a corporate-level restructuring of the group has led to a changed role for this division and it needs to work out its new priorities and how to organise to refocus on these.

The need in these contexts is for a fundamental and organisation-wide review of its situation and options, developing a new strategic plan from the changed circumstances in which the organisation finds itself. One approach to this is to assess the organisation's current position and the implications for its future from three perspectives:

- What is happening externally, in its industry and markets, and what might change significantly in the future?
- What are its capabilities as an organisation, and how might these affect its ability to succeed?
- What should be the purpose and driving focus of the organisation, and how should its people work together to realise this?

To begin to answer these questions we can focus the first stage of the strategic planning process on these three areas: the external industry and market environment, the organisation's capabilities and what its role and purpose should be. And we can break down the first fundamental question, 'Where are we now?' into more focused questions that define the working briefs for those involved in the groups or workstreams that might be set up to tackle these topics.

We will come back shortly to how these workstreams interrelate, but first let us drill further down to some of the more detailed questions that the 'market' workgroup could consider (Figure 5.5).

In a similar way it could consider 'our industry' – looking at the industry structure, competitors and some of the influences on these – and 'our products (or services)', considering the current portfolio and how well it is positioned in the market and how this might change.

Taking a step back from the detail, what I have tried to illustrate through this example is how questions can be used at every level to help stimulate and guide the thinking; appropriately framed, they can provide the starting point for people to gather the data and insights that would be useful to inform the discussion and also the encouragement to probe and challenge established ways of looking at the situation, leading to new ways of thinking.

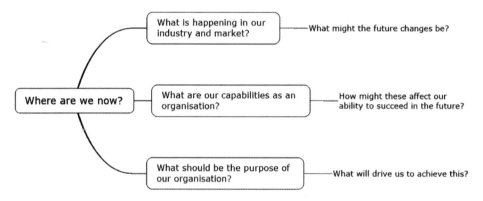

Figure 5.4 Where are we now?

Figure 5.5 Asking the questions

These questions evolve as the thinking progresses (rather than being predefined); it is an iterative process, driven by the search for meaning, to fully understand something – put simply, the need to make sense of things. A particular line of enquiry can prompt further questions, until sufficient understanding is achieved for what is required to be able to answer the question at the level relevant at this time.

Another very important point: it's not for those who are planning the overall strategy journey to define the specific detailed questions within the broader framework, but for the people directly involved in such detail at that time. The art and skill of leadership within a strategic planning process is to create the environment and provide the stimulus, the encouragement and the challenge to enable people to work out for themselves what are the questions they need to answer to develop a shared understanding about the higher-level question posed originally. It is they who will then drive the quest for information, for insights, to develop robust answers that make sense of what was asked and to be able to explain these confidently to others.

Meetings, meetings, meetings . . .

. . . and Awaydays. Board workshops at secluded country hotels, breakout sessions with flipcharts, the rushed end-of day group feedback sessions. Trying to pick out the strategy nuggets afterwards from the pages of indecipherable marker pen bullet points. A perhaps too-familiar scenario replicated in so many traditional strategic plan processes?

Alternatively, there is strategic planning managed like an IT project. Detailed deliverables and deadlines for every step, reports to steering groups and sponsors that focus on traffic light assessments of progress against a predefined timetable (with opportunities to share understanding swamped by the debate about justifications for each of the red, amber or green dots on the project plan).

Let us remind ourselves about what's at the heart of strategic planning – namely people and their need to make sense of where their organisation is currently and where it's going. And that it is the quality and depth of the conversations they have that lead to this understanding. The art of strategic planning is to encourage such conversations to take place.

When approached with this philosophy, every meeting has the potential to be a constructive part of this development – whether it's a board workshop or a spontaneous catch-up conversation at the coffee machine. The Awayday can be planned to enable thinking to be shared, clarified, challenged and developed or decisions to be taken about strategy and priorities. The regular steering group report can concentrate on where people working on the various focus areas have got to in their thinking and what help they might need to make progress with any difficulties. The coffee machine conversation needs no planning, just a mutual desire to exchange views and think about what was said.

Organising the opportunities for such conversations is part of the art of planning the journey; the challenge is to find ways to balance the aim of wide involvement with ensuring focus and effectiveness of the process – in all but the smallest organisations it is not possible to include everyone in every discussion. Complex or difficult subjects requiring deeper consideration are likely to be more effectively discussed in smaller groups; in a larger group there will be more individual perspectives and approaches and it will be more difficult to achieve a consensus for how the conversation should proceed.

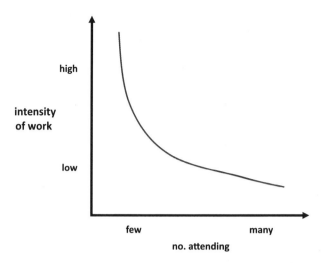

Figure 5.6 Intensity and focus

Choosing the type of meeting that is likely to be most effective for the intensity of work required is an aspect of the 'leadership' required in a strategy journey. This includes thinking about what inputs are required, the location and style of meeting, as well as who should attend. As with all meetings, clear communication in advance of the purpose of the meeting together with well-organised and relevant information to provide the context will help attendees come prepared to engage, having started to 'tune in' their thinking to the subject matter. Explaining to people what to expect and what is expected from the discussion helps people make sense of the purpose of the meeting and how it fits into the overall strategic planning process.

Similar forward thinking is needed about what might follow this, how this will fit with the series of conversations required to ensure the thinking is shared, understood, refined and adopted. Is this a development phase of the thinking or about communicating what has been developed? Where does it fit into decision-making or adoption of an idea? Who else needs to be consulted as part of this process?

Such thinking is (or should be) part of the usual way of working within an organisation – it is essential common sense and good practice! However, a strategy journey is a different sort of process to the usual operational and transaction-focused agendas and established formal meeting structures; there are more unknowns, deeper waters of thinking to explore and more strands to consider and coordinate – and hence seemingly more complex a process. So there is more thinking to be done to enable the many rich conversations needed along the journey.

I am wary of the impression this might give of the need to plan a strategic planning process in the utmost detail, to mastermind a thorough plan of meetings, workshops, reports, updates and briefings that drives the organisation through the various stages. But as you might recall from the example I used in the introduction that helped develop my approach to strategic planning, it is more a journey of discovery, an adventure embarked upon by the organisation over terrain that is at best only sketchily mapped,

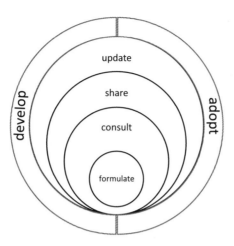

Figure 5.7 Objectives of meetings

rather than a chauffeured drive along a motorway. The aim of the prior discussion is to illustrate some of the thinking required in planning and navigating a strategy journey; it is about thinking ahead, considering what the outcomes might be and what next steps might be required, who needs to be involved and how best to enable this, what the implications might be and how to deal with these. Considering the next move in a chess game is a closer analogy: what the options are, which pieces to bring into play, what might happen as a result and whether this is the optimum move to make at this time. As in chess, there needs to be flexibility to adapt to what actually happens next, to rethink through the ensuing stages if necessary; planning and navigating a strategy journey is a dynamic process. The key strategic leadership attribute required is to be able to think this through – what's right for the process now, what might be the next steps – and to have the confidence to be able to adapt this as the journey evolves, rather than to manage a pre-planned process however thoroughly it's been thought through. We shall explore some of the aspects of navigating a strategy journey later in this chapter.

Opportunities to share the thinking are an essential aspect of the strategy journey. In the previous section we focused on the work of those focusing on a specific key area and how well-framed questions can stimulate this. We will now look at the need to bring together the work from these various groups to help develop a platform for the next stage.

To illustrate this we will return to our example of the organisation undertaking a fundamental reassessment of its strategy. To answer the question 'Where are we now?' it set up three workstreams: one looking at the external market and industry picture, one considering the internal capabilities of the organisation and one re-examining the organisation's purpose and aims. The thinking that is being developed in each group has implications for the other areas. For instance, a market development strategy that relies on capabilities that the organisation does not currently possess cannot be achieved without a strategic decision being taken to invest in acquiring these. Similarly an option of low-cost manufacturing to enable the organisation to enter a commodity sector will be inconsistent with a strategy of focusing on building on the organisation's research and development strengths and concentrating on high-value, innovative, technologically advanced products.

Sharing the thinking as it develops across the three workstreams is therefore important in providing context and informing the ensuing work of each group. However, it does not necessarily mean that some of the ideas being developed in a particular workstream have to be rejected automatically, just that they need to acknowledge the potential inconsistency. (It is also possible that the thinking changes and the ideas are no longer inconsistent.)

However, there will be a stage in the process in which the thinking about these areas needs to be brought together in order to progress to developing consistent strategies and consequent options for the organisation to consider and decide upon. This synthesis of the thinking developed by each workstream is a vital step in the strategy journey; it is the forum for summarising an assessment of the current position of the organisation and its prospects and the crucible for developing coherent and viable strategies and articulating their implications as the basis for debate and decision-making. Taking our example a stage further, it might be appropriate to construct alternative options of a low-cost manufacturing, high-volume low-margin products strategy and one of high-value low-volume sales

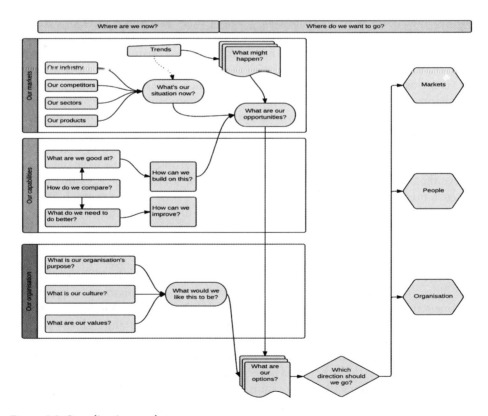

Figure 5.8 Coordinating workstreams

of technologically advanced products; the challenge at this stage is to crystallise coherent strategically consistent options to inform further discussion. Whatever is decided about the strategy options will of course inform the next stage of the strategy journey, including further development of the implications across all the workstream areas.

Figure 5.8 illustrates this example, showing how the work of the three groups is brought together to enable a platform to be created for the next stage of the journey.

When planning this strategy journey the need will have been identified to build such a step into the process at this stage. In thinking about 'Who's interested?' it will also have been clear that board (or equivalent governing body) would need to be involved in this strategy debate and subsequent decision-making; other groups or individuals will need to be considered too so they are aware of the thinking that has developed and can contribute as appropriate to this.

So this is one of the stages where opportunities need to be planned for people to meet to enable this thinking to be explained and shared and discussed and decisions taken about how to move on. Maybe the board needs an Awayday after all – but is that enough, and how can 'decision by flipchart' be avoided?

Time and space

So, what should be arranged to facilitate the types of conversations necessary to deliberate with due thoroughness the various strategic directions the organisation could take?

First, everyone involved needs to have a deep understanding of the thinking that has led to these strategy options. To gain this they will need to go through their own individual thinking processes to make sense of it for themselves. This does not mean of course that they have to replicate all the work undertaken by the workstreams in getting to this point, but it does require working through the rationale, supported by relevant information – and having the opportunity to challenge and test this.

When people are trying to understand something new we often hear them use phrases like 'I need to tune into the subject', 'I need to get my brain into gear', 'I'm still trying to get my head around it' and 'I'm working through what it means in my own mind'. These are clear signals about the individual thinking processes that are going on, which are essential to enable someone to grasp an argument and fully understand it – to the extent that they can think for themselves about the consequences and implications. Attempting to short-cut or by-pass this mental process results in people feeling uneasy about their understanding – not because the logic might be flawed, but simply because their brains have not yet had the opportunity to work through this and test it out for themselves. Although someone in a group might appear to accede to persuasion from the group to collectively accept the argument so they can move on, such a step can leave that person with a sense of unease and may hinder their ability to work out the consequences. If it is about something as important as the organisation's future strategic direction then this is an unsatisfactory position to be in for both the individual and the organisation.

Appreciating just how important this process is in achieving understanding is part of the leadership skills required on a strategy journey; this applies just as much to the colleagues in a group that is working through how to answer a strategy question as to those guiding the organisation on its strategy journey.

The implications of this in planning a strategy journey are significant. Returning to the example of organising the opportunity for the board to consider which strategic direction the organisation should pursue, it is now apparent that this will not be achieved just by arranging a board workshop. The thinking underpinning these options will need to be explained to them; the individual board members will need time to digest this and work through their own mental processes to make sense of the reasoning; they need the opportunity to discuss and clarify their interpretation and to question and challenge any points about which they are uncertain. There then will need to be given the opportunity for collective discussion and consideration of the strategic options, with the space to work through these as a group to ensure there is a shared understanding about what they mean. The next step is of course debate and decision-making, and if opinion is divided there might need to be further work undertaken before a decision is made. The concluding step at this time is to discuss how their decision will affect what happens in the next stage of the strategy journey.

So we can see that there are several steps involved in the board coming to a decision, and due space needs to be allowed in the process to enable these to occur. In our example it might be that this is organised as follows:

1   Board members read about the context and an explanation of the thinking in a briefing document that they receive several days before they meet.
2   A workshop is arranged at which those from the workstreams involved in developing these strategies explain and discuss their thinking with the board (and any others invited). Discussions are aimed at obtaining clarity and developing shared understanding about what is meant, including questions and challenges to test the robustness of the thinking (which might prompt further work in response).
3   There's a space allowed for people to think further about these strategies, seek and obtain any further clarifications, express any concerns and doubts. (This space could be a few days or several weeks, depending on the depth or complexity of the thinking, the need to work through implications or evaluate the different options and the potential impact on the organisation.)
4   Steps 1 and 2 could be repeated in one or more iterations.
5   The final step is to meet and share where each person has arrived in their thinking, to have the depth of discussion and 'rich conversations' to achieve a clear understanding of each individual's interpretation and views and to begin the process of coming to a decision about how to progress.

The intention in going through this example in some detail is not to spell out a precise process, but to illustrate the need to allow time for such thinking and discussion. Appreciating the mental processes that people go through to achieve understanding and to work out meaning and implications, and the need for rich conversations to help in this, is important in considering the real nature of a strategy journey and how to guide this.

In the fast-moving pace of our working lives we are not accustomed to this. The drive to act, to get things done, to respond and resolve quickly, to achieve results is ingrained in our organisations. We struggle to create the time and the 'brain space' to think more deeply, and we do not find the opportunity for the conversations that help us develop our thinking and share it with others.

Another phrase: 'I haven't had the time to think about it'. And 'We don't spend enough time thinking about strategy' (or discussing it). A strategy journey needs to create that opportunity to enable and encourage people and the organisation to seek to understand what the future of their organisation might be.

There is a fine balance to achieve in managing the pace of the journey, between the desire to conclude it successfully as soon as possible whilst appreciating the time it will take for people to take the steps along the path as they travel together.

Navigating

A group of people meet to plan a journey of exploration and pore over what sketchy maps have been created by previous travellers. Some parts of the journey would appear to be straightforward, and everybody expects progress there to be brisk, whilst there is little information about what the terrain might be like for other stretches. The path appears only vaguely defined in places, and it looks as though the party will need to find a way across these sections when it gets there. Despite this, there is great confidence within the group that they can maintain a good pace throughout – the weather forecast seems favourable, and people are optimistic about completing the journey in good time.

One or two of the more experienced travellers harbour some doubts that the journey will proceed according to plan without some unforeseen delay or obstacles on the way, and they know that everyone in the party will not be able to sustain the ambitious pace throughout. Keeping together is important – splitting into smaller groups going at different paces will leave the overall expedition exposed to more risks. But others are keen to press ahead and aim to make good time.

A strategy journey (based on an actual case from my personal experience): the context was challenging, involving two groups with different perspectives developing a joint view of the future. In the initial planning about how they expected the journey to go a milestone was set for completion of the first phase, together with a view about the anticipated output from this. The phrase 'completing Document X by Month Y' soon became established as the target to be achieved.

But this was not what happened. It took some time for the two groups to learn how they could work together and to share and understand each other's perspectives. They struggled to find a way of describing the overall picture bringing together these perspectives in a way to which both could relate as a basis for working out how change could occur. Gradually they created a framework for expressing this that made sense to them both, and from that point they had a common basis they could use to develop their shared thinking.

As Month Y approached, it was clear that there would be no Document X. However, what had been achieved was that the groups had found a way in which they could work together to begin to develop a joint view about the strategic options for future development, with the momentum increasing as the thinking started to take shape. They had discovered their own path across some difficult terrain. The leadership response to this was to recognise this as a successful route forward and to encourage future progress, rather than to criticise for the failure to deliver what had been expected by the original deadline.

Being flexible enough to adapt is an important aspect of navigating a journey. Progress can be hampered if difficult terrain is encountered, or if detours are needed around obstacles, and there can be other deviations from the planned route and occasionally some blind alleys.

Neither the rate of progress nor the route of a strategy journey is likely to be linear. As we saw in the illustration of the process by which a board might make a decision about which strategic direction to pursue, it might take more than one attempt to achieve the level of common understanding required. Further work might be required on working through the implications of each option – for example, modelling how the financial projections might change in a different scenario. It can often take several drafts to refine a strategy statement until it expresses precisely what is intended; summaries of analyses can be improved so key points are highlighted; several drafts of a strategic plan document will be reviewed before the final version; early attempts to make sense of a situation can be discarded as the thinking develops; and fresh insights can lead to revised inferences. This iterative approach is characteristic of a process of trying to make sense of a situation, of testing the understanding of shared meaning and finding ways of expressing this so it can be understood throughout the organisation.

It is achieving this understanding that is important, and this seldom happens just by a pre-planned process, but through a series of conversations by which meaning is clarified and shared. For example, in the case of one of the workstreams we mentioned earlier the original plan might have been to tackle the work in four fortnightly meetings of those involved. However, during the discussion in the first meeting the team concluded that there were two distinct aspects that needed to be considered more fully, and it was agreed to set up two smaller workgroups to report back at the next meeting. These might also consult other people for clarification or ideas, and if further work in these groups proved necessary it might be decided not to proceed with one of the planned workstream meetings. So as Figure 5.9 illustrates, the actual path of conversations could be very different to the original plan of four meetings.

Amongst the most challenging aspects of a strategic planning process to navigate are the people dynamics – individual and group attitudes and behaviours, their level

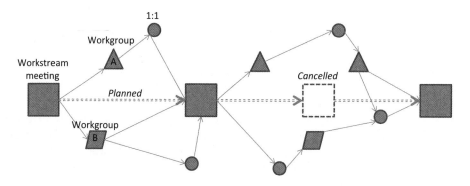

Figure 5.9 Workstream paths

of engagement and support and the many relationships involved over the duration of a strategy journey. The importance of the subject – the future of the organisation and the implications for the people in it – means the stakes are high, with much at risk if the thinking is flawed. But also the process can challenge established views and threaten people's roles and influence; people and groups can engage in the process at political and emotional levels, as well as the rational.

Leadership in a strategy journey requires astute awareness of such dynamics and the confidence and ability to handle them. Emotional intelligence and empathy are needed as much as strategic thinking, perceptive analysis and persistent rationality, with acutely sensitive antennae detecting fluctuations in levels of engagement, commitment or support. Much of this leadership happens away from the main path of the journey, with conversations and other interventions to explore concerns or dissent, to reassure or to encourage full participation. Strategic planning is about people, and its traditional perceptions as a dry, analytical and sometimes soulless exercise belie the importance of the leadership aspects of the process. More time, thought and energy can be spent on engaging with people than on developing the content: get the former right and the latter will follow.

Agreeing on the principles and rules for the journey at the outset can be a very useful way of keeping everyone together *en route*, and well-articulated frameworks for specific activities help set a clear brief. For example, in a comparison of customer service with competitors an explicit statement of the principle that these have to take a customer perspective can be used to challenge any attempt to defend current performance and reassert the need for an objective approach.

Navigating is also about anticipating and thinking ahead about what might happen on the journey. Like chess, considering how to deal with various options a few moves ahead can inform how the immediate next steps are handled. To use our real journey analogy, anticipating that yesterday's rain might cause difficulties traversing a river in two days' time means that you can make contingency preparations. In strategy development, if you can foresee that the implications of a particular line of thinking might provoke concerns in a part of the organisation, then you can work to ensure that this is communicated sensitively and emphasised that it is as an exploratory option and not a decision.

There can be times when the journey falters. The challenge of resolving a strategic issue might be too daunting; the options identified might be politically untenable (for example pessimistic financial implications or requiring major job losses); people might lose heart or feel their contribution is not fully appreciated or taken into account. Anticipating these before they can bring the journey to a halt is not always possible. Navigating such obstacles requires courage; if the route being taken is heading towards an impasse, then it is clear that some rethinking is necessary to regroup and set off on an alternative path. This might mean stopping work in some areas and starting anew with a different brief or perhaps pausing the overall process whilst key issues are clarified (for example, decisions might be taken to rule out particular options, after which the work recommences with a restated brief).

This adapting, flexible, dynamic approach to navigating the strategy journey requires some important leadership attributes: the ability to plan each stage but also to modify this, sometimes quite radically; the awareness of people in the organisation and their perspectives, including recognising that engaging in a strategic planning process can cause apprehension and that uncertainty can be uncomfortable; thinking ahead and considering alternative routes whilst keeping in sight the intended destination. All these require confidence and a focus on the people and the journey.

In this chapter we have seen how the reasons for developing a strategic plan at a particular time can influence the approach taken and how thinking about some of the key areas that need to be addressed helps in planning the process. Considering what interest and influence various groups of people have in the development of the organisation's strategic plan will help map out a framework for how and when they are involved, including identifying some key decision points along the way.

We looked at how well-framed questions can drive the process, stimulating the thinking and providing a brief for the strategising and organising work involved in developing a strategic plan. Understanding how people make sense of situations and develop their understanding led to an appreciation of the importance of allowing the time and space for this to happen, and I propounded the idea that the art of planning and guiding a strategic planning process lies in enabling and encouraging 'rich conversations' of the depth and quality that lead to shared understanding. Meetings and workshops are just two of the vehicles for these.

We concluded the chapter by considering some of the aspects and challenges of navigating a strategy journey, including the need to anticipate and think ahead; we also emphasised the importance of leadership and how investing time and energy engaging with people is as essential a part of this as developing the content of a strategic plan.

6

THE CONTENT

In chapters 4 and 5 we looked at two of the 'dimensions' of strategic planning. We considered why it was important to understand the *context* in which the strategic plan was being developed, including the reason why an organisation would decide to undertake this at that particular time. We saw how the context influenced the approach taken in planning the *process* and explored the power of questions, the importance of conversations and some of the challenges of navigating a strategy journey. The fundamental theme running through all of these is that people are at the heart of strategic planning.

In this chapter we will explore the third dimension of strategic planning, the *content*. First, a definition: by 'content' I include everything that is produced as a result of a strategic planning process that captures some of the key information or thinking involved and that is useful to the organisation in developing, communicating or implementing its strategic plan.

This is a significantly broader definition than just the 'strategic plan document' that is the customary focal point in the traditional view of strategic planning. I have argued earlier in the book just how limiting such a focus can be. In adopting a more extensive perspective we are being consistent with the defining statement we developed in chapter 3:

> *Strategic planning is how the people in an organisation make sense of where it's going and how it's going to get there.*

Our definition of the content includes all the outputs from the strategic planning process that help with this.

Just to be clear, I am not envisaging a large physical filing system labelled 'Strategic Plan Content' which contains the written records from every stage, every meeting, every decision during the development of the strategic plan. These three dimensions of strategic planning are concepts rather than physical entities. Just as context relates to all the factors in an organisation's current situation that might influence how it goes about its strategic planning at this time, and process refers to every aspect of planning and navigating such an organisational journey, so content includes all the information, ideas, outcomes from discussion and so on, whether written or not, that have helped or will help the organisation with this journey.

So, this chapter is not about defining the format and contents of an ideal strategic plan document (we shall consider in chapter 7 how we might approach this). Nor is it about a comprehensive categorisation of all the content that could fit within our broad definition of the concept. We shall focus instead on how we can develop some of the most helpful content.

Information and insight

What information do you need to develop a strategic plan? There are two approaches that are commonly used in collecting this from across the organisation:

- *Vacuum cleaner*: a comprehensive sweep up of every piece of data that might be useful, compiling an impressive reference library of source material that can be accessed at any stage
- *Fill in the boxes*: tables of the required information are predefined, and departments are tasked with providing specific data to complete their part of it.

The 'vacuum cleaner' approach is similar to that used by some management consultancies: engaged by their client to undertake a review of a particular area (product range, manufacturing, productivity and so on), the first stage of the process includes gathering up all the available data, with boxes of reports and Gigabytes of electronic files transported to their offices where teams of graduate trainees will spend hours of their evenings sorting through for anything that supports the developing case to be made. This is then used as sources for the impressive analysis presented in their final report, although how the information was used is not transparent; it is not possible for people in the organisation to check whether its use in this context is valid.

There are similar risks with this approach in strategic planning, although it should be easier in this case for people in the organisation to check with their colleagues that a particular use of the data is appropriate. One advantage of the vacuum cleaner approach is that some of the information that is likely to be used in developing the strategic plan is readily accessible, avoiding frustrating delays in requesting it from departments busy with 'the day job'; however, there can still be a disconnect with those providing the information not also determining its use and ensuring it is interpreted correctly.

A 'fill in the boxes' approach also has disconnection risks. In this case, whilst it is clear what specific data is required, it might not be apparent to those providing it why it has been requested. This is unlikely to be a problem when this is standard information that is used regularly within the organisation; however, if its intended use is to help understand a particular issue, an opportunity could be missed to provide other information that would be helpful as well.

Of course, each of these approaches is valid when used appropriately; collecting standard reports or filling in templates with regularly reported data can be efficient ways of gathering information to support the planning process. However, there is another approach which can be very effective, especially in the search for understanding and insights.

In chapter 5 we highlighted just how powerful questions could be in a strategic planning process, helping focus the thinking and provide an effective brief for the work. To answer a question the first step is to think through the various aspects of it, the constituent parts that will contribute to formulating an answer. This leads to identifying the types of information needed about these component aspects and triggers the search for where such information might be found. And when searching for this from new sources there might be other related information available that can enhance understanding. This inquisitive, 'discovery' approach also stimulates ideas about new ways of looking at a situation, which can lead to a deeper understanding and creative ways of responding to this.

Whilst this might seem to be a rational, common-sense approach, it is remarkable that it is seldom applied to its full potential. In the hectic action-driven rush of most working days the approach to information is likely to be 'sufficient for what's needed now', good enough to provide a basis for completion of a task or for making a pressing decision. There is neither time nor need to explore or investigate further.

However, strategic planning does require those insights which can lead to deeper understanding. We need to give our minds permission to be enquiring, to explore and investigate. As mentioned in chapter 5 one of the leadership challenges of those planning and guiding the strategy journey is to facilitate and encourage such enquiry. Generating the space and time for this to happen is one aspect of this; equally important is creating the right climate and encouraging an enquiring mindset to develop.

Challenge has a role to play in this. It's a continual series of testing the validity of assumptions, logical arguments and conclusions, whether conducted by oneself ('What evidence do I have for this?' 'Is that really what this chart is telling me?') or others ('Could an alternative conclusion be . . .?' 'Is that consistent with . . .?').

Incisive analysis is important and involves applying relentless logic and ruthless questioning of conclusions, driving down several levels to pinpoint the root cause of a problem or the critical lever of influence. Also essential is understanding the limitations of data. A couple of examples to illustrate these points (both are set in a healthcare context, but the points made apply more generally):

1   Hospitals have traditionally planned the number of beds they will need based on the average (mean) number of days that patients stay in hospital. Hospital A was facing financial pressures and had decided it needed to improve its operational efficiencies as one of the principal strategic objectives in its strategic plan for the next three years. One initiative suggested at an early stage of the strategic planning process was to increase its bed occupancy rates (reducing the amount of time over the year when beds were classed as 'unoccupied'; this included the time needed to discharge patients, change the bed linen, clean the bed bay and admit the next patient). Analysis of ward data was presented to the working group that was considering this. It showed that there was scope to increase occupancy rates whilst still leaving some contingency after allowing for 'patient changeover time'. A strong financial case was presented that showed this would have a significant positive impact on the hospital's finances, and there was pressure to implement this as an 'early win'.

Despite this, one member of the working group felt uneasy about the proposal and persuaded her colleagues to undertake some further modelling. She suggested that the group commission a statistical analysis of patient length-of-stay durations, looking at the range of variation as well as the average; her desire to understand this prompted her to read some papers about capacity planning, and she recommended to the group that they model what would happen at various occupancy rates before any decision was made. The outcome of this

63

(and the extensive debates that followed) was not only that the proposal to increase occupancy rates was rejected, but that the hospital started recording additional data about bed occupancy and defined an upper limit as policy.

2   The waiting list for patients requiring an operation was growing at Hospital B. It had a full schedule of sessions booked in its operating theatres, although some of these had to be cancelled, usually because a previous case had overrun or because there was no bed available in the intensive care ward for the patient immediately after the operation. The surgeons were lobbying hard for the hospital to invest in an additional theatre; the intensive care staff complained that there were not enough beds available in the general wards to move their patients to when they no longer need intensive care (so freeing up beds for post-operative patients); and the ward managers were frustrated because of delays in discharging patients back home, either because the consultants didn't complete their ward rounds in time or because there were delays in arranging family or social care support for patients for when they returned home. Did the hospital need to invest in more theatre capacity, more intensive care beds, more ward beds or a combination of these?

It was clear that this required a systems-thinking approach and determined analysis at a number of levels (particularly the patient flows between the parts of the system). It was also acknowledged that it was a complex and challenging problem; as well as the need for thorough analysis there were several different 'stakeholder' groups involved, some of whom held strong opinions about who or what was to blame. In considering the strategic planning context, this was one of the most pressing problems facing the hospital, and the solution (whatever it was) would be an important initiative in the hospital's strategic plan (affecting its capital programme and its future activity projections).

Planning the strategic planning process for this hospital, the importance and complexity of this, plus the need to engage all the various stakeholders, pointed to the need to tackle this in advance of when key decisions needed to be made about the overall strategic plan. The hospital recognised the importance of this and chose to invest in external help with the expertise to analyse the situation, using operational research, systems thinking and statistical analysis skills. This was the only additional investment that the hospital made, apart from the time to engage with all the stakeholders throughout the process, informing and educating them as the analysis progressed. The solution lay in a parallel series of initiatives across all component parts of the system, mostly involving flows – patients, information and how people communicate. Putting this into practice was one of the key strategic initiatives included in the organisation's strategic plan later that year.

This fictional example illustrates the value of considering strategic planning as a strategy journey for an organisation; there was leadership, strategising (in the form of in-depth thinking to inform decision-making), organising (planning how this would be tackled, including involving everyone interested), and learning (the organisation, and key groups of peoples within it, gained an understanding about systems thinking and how to tackle complex problems).

It also demonstrates the important role that analysis can play in informing the thinking that goes into developing such a strategic plan.

Let us use the example of a 'markets' workstream (similar to the illustration used in chapter 5) that is trying to understand where the organisation's products fit into the market. There will probably be established ways of dividing the market into sectors and measuring each product's market share. The data can be analysed to show the relative growth trend of each sector and how the product shares have changed; whatever is deduced about the trends can be used to guide assumptions about the future and hence to develop projections for the sales of the company's products if there were no major changes affecting the market.

But such analysis does not give any insight into why these trends are happening or what innovations might change the dynamics of the market. The supplementary question in our illustration in chapter 5 asked, 'Are there any other ways of looking at this market?' Finding the answer to this could lead to a change in strategy.

There is an excellent example of this from my own experience early in my career. In the UK biscuit market in the 1980s the established way of looking at the market was in sectors defined by the sweetness of the biscuit (sweet, semi-sweet, plain and so on), and analysing a product's performance in these sectors was the customary way of setting the context for considering future strategy as well as determining the assumptions used to develop sales projections. However, at this particular time United Biscuits, which was the biggest player in the UK market, started a strategic planning initiative to consider its longer-term prospects including its product portfolio and any implications for its manufacturing capacity. This prompted a deeper consideration about the UK biscuit market and what might be influencing the trends; although the marketing analysis was thorough and quite sophisticated, it was apparent that this yielded no insights into what was influencing these trends. Unless the company could develop a better understanding of this and could change its strategy accordingly there was a strong likelihood that decisions about closing factories might be made on the basis of extrapolating current sales trends.

What happened next had a major impact on United Biscuits's fortunes over the next few years. Realising the importance of what it didn't know, it commissioned research into exploring in some depth what people thought about biscuits and how they used them. From the resulting information it was able to develop a creative new way of segmenting the market based on the different ways people used the various types of biscuit and how they perceived them. This was used as a basis for considering the current product range and in changing the product portfolio strategy accordingly. Importantly it was able to identify an opportunity to launch a new product into one of the market spaces defined in the new segmentation model; the success of this, McVitie's Hobnobs, provided a vital sales boost at what had been a pivotal time.

This example illustrates the importance of insights in informing strategy. Making sense of information can be a stimulating process of discovery, of thinking about different ways in which it could be interpreted; finding new insights from this is challenging and requires being creative with the lenses through which the information is considered, trying various hypothetical models and testing whether the data might support these. We have seen how questions can drive the search for relevant information and encourage incisive analysis; the desire to make sense of situations, to understand what the key dynamics are, is a powerful motivator to seek new insights.

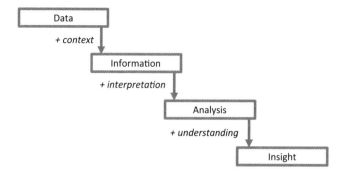

Figure 6.1 Information and insights (the hidden depths of data)

Tools and techniques

This is a book about 'strategic planning'. Strategic planning is associated with complex analyses and sophisticated strategy development techniques. Therefore, what should follow in this section is an overview of several of the more commonly used tools and an indication of when to use them.

Except it doesn't.

This is a book about 'strategy journeys'. Strategy journeys are about how people make sense of how their organisation should develop and decide how they are going to help make this happen. Strategy journeys are about exploration, discovery and learning, as well as about choices and well-informed decisions. They are about how people talk, share ideas and work together to shape their organisation's future.

So this section is about what tools and techniques can help with this, with the emphasis on content (information or thinking developed during the strategy journey which is useful to the organisation in developing, communicating or implementing its strategic plan).

Thinking in 2-D

There are a lot of diagrams in this book. I hope they help illustrate and reinforce some of the points I have made in the text (for some readers they might be more effective!). There is a reason for this: pictures can be very helpful in conveying information and ideas, and I use them often to try to crystallise my thinking and convey it to others. 'Pictures' in this sense include diagrams, charts, grids, two-by-two matrices (or matrices of any other dimension) – anything that represents information visually rather than just by words.

One of the concepts in NLP (neurolinguistic programming) is that individuals vary in their use of different 'sensory channels', and this can be conveyed in the words they tend to use to express themselves. Some people seem to prefer visual channels (clues are in their use of phrases like 'I can picture that' and 'that looks fine'); for others the auditory channel is used frequently ('That sounds like a good idea', 'That rings a bell'), and some are more kinaesthetic in their language, with feelings and touch featuring in their phrases ('I feel that's right', 'I can touch success'). Most people use all of these (and there are also other less frequently used sensory channels), but many have a preferred channel that they use more often.

By expressing ideas pictorially people can use their visual sensory channel to help interpret and understand these ideas. Similarly, using sensory channel language in conversations can make thinking more accessible. Techniques that help others understand the intended meaning more easily are part of the art of encouraging 'rich conversations' within a strategy journey.

Diagrams can be a very effective tool in strategic planning discussions, helping develop and clarify ideas. Unlike text or bullet points, a 2-D representation enables people to see the relationships between the various elements, whether these are different aspects of a concept or model, processes or flows or a series of sequential events. Graphs and charts of course are pictorial formats that help people interpret data; the use of two-by-two grids to help position or categorise information is a well-established strategic analysis tool (although two by two is the most frequently used version, the grid can be of any reasonable size, and not necessarily square; it is the two-dimensional view that makes this effective).

Drawing a diagram whilst trying to explain an idea can help others understand the reasoning – it's a form of animated visual to accompany the words being spoken. As you try to express your ideas, drawing the way you see things, people are following your reasoning step by step. Even if the final drawing ends up as a mess of scribbles unintelligible to anyone seeing it for the first time, those who have watched and listened as you have been drawing and explaining will almost certainly have a good understanding of the ideas you were wanting to convey. (The popularity of courses teaching cartooning in a business context and of videos using animated cartoon drawings illustrate that this is seen as an effective technique to communicate a topic or argument.)

Some examples . . .

Perhaps the most commonly used strategic analysis grid is SWOT – strengths, weaknesses, opportunities, threats. It is a powerful tool, summarising the organisation's own assessment of its current situation. Beneath the simplicity of the labels for the individual grid squares (or cells) are two dimensions that prompt the all-round assessment of the organisation: an internal-external axis and a present-future axis.

Figure 6.2 SWOT

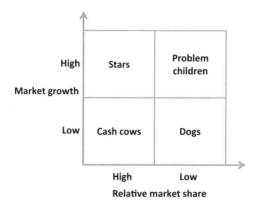

Figure 6.3 Boston Consulting Group portfolio analysis matrix

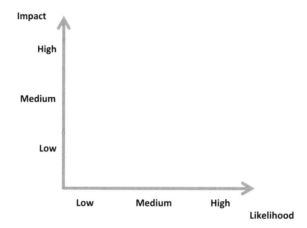

Figure 6.4 Risk assessment grid

SWOT is obviously well established and widely used, and there are numerous other proven tools to analyse particular aspects. Two more examples are the Boston Consulting Group portfolio analysis matrix used to assess the prospects for products or business units, and hence help the organisation decide its future strategy for them, and the impact-likelihood grid for mapping risks. (Strictly speaking – mathematically – these are grids, not matrices, but we will let that pass and stick with the names that are in common use!).

There are of course many others, but my purpose in including the three examples here is not because they are amongst the most widely used, but to illustrate the power of well-chosen axes. The aim of this book is to help demystify strategic planning and explain how to approach it from a 'first principles' perspective, to encourage people to develop the capability and confidence to embark on strategy journeys in their own organisations. Representing ideas, explaining thinking, enabling rich conversations that help develop, elucidate and share meaning – all are part of the armoury of tools that can be used. Working out how to look at a situation, how to analyse it and how best to express this thinking is one aspect of this, including finding the most helpful way to show the situation in a way that will explain, clarify or stimulate others' thinking.

Deciding what this should be can be a combination of trial and error and inspiration. Often there is a lot of 'playing around' with the information, toying with looking at it in various ways, before an idea starts to form that seems promising. In choosing the axes to use in grids it helps to work out what factors are most fundamental, which are the key differentiators or what attributes are most influential (for example, what matters to customers; what characterises the players in a sector?). Although this is a way of analysing information in a strategy development process, in some respects it also requires creative thinking to tease out ways of considering that might lead to insights and deeper understanding. And like all creative processes, sometimes it doesn't work – there are no patterns to see, no meaningful conclusions to be drawn, nothing that will be useful to inform the strategising. In which case, if it is relevant but unrevealing, it is useful information to be retained for reference, whilst moving on to try other approaches or consider other analyses as potential sources of insight.

In chapter 5 we discussed the importance of allowing time and space for thinking to develop. Strategising in particular requires this. First, we need to achieve as clear a picture as we can of what is important about the organisation's current situation and what we think could affect its future. We are looking for new insights that might help us with this and ways of communicating our thinking that help others contribute to developing such a picture and resonate with them as making sense. The content we generate during this analysis phase of strategising is a vital platform on which we will develop strategies for the future. In every strategy journey with which I have been involved there is usually one particular piece of work developed during this process that is especially powerful and that then has a significant influence on the formation of strategy. It might be a new insight, a different way of considering a situation, that then provides a framework or reference for developing strategy (for example, in the United Biscuits example I described earlier in this chapter the insight they developed into consumers' attitudes to the various types of biscuits, why they bought them and how they used them, formed the framework within which the company developed its strategy for the next five years).

Iteration, iteration, iteration

We have noted that a 'try it and see if it works' approach might be required in developing strategic analyses, to probe the information for insights and to find ways of expressing this that help share the thinking and stimulate others' contribution. This approach, of exploration and discovery, is different to much of the day-to-day style of work in most organisations, which tends to be transactional communication of information and operational decision-making and action. To encourage people to think and talk in a more strategic way, to develop understanding rather than determine actions, requires a change in thinking style. Creating the time, space and environment to enable this to develop and flourish is one of the leadership challenges in guiding an organisation along its strategy journey. We discussed in chapter 5 some of the thinking that might go into organising such opportunities: gathering together the right people; choosing a location with the space and ambience conducive to this style of thinking and conversation; providing guidance through a well-thought-through brief, ideally question led, with relevant inputs to inform the discussion. There is another technique that I want to introduce here that can be very helpful in developing the content from this strategising process; it is simple and somewhat obvious, but also remarkably effective.

Meetings have outcomes. Ideally they have structures that facilitate these outcomes – topics are discussed according to an agenda, decisions and agreed-upon actions are noted in minutes and then progress is reviewed at the next relevant opportunity. Here, the content is a documented record of what has been discussed and what has been agreed upon, precise and actionable. Whilst of course not all topic discussions reach neat conclusions (nor are all meetings ideal!), this approach befits the operational nature of making things happen in organisations.

However, as we have seen, the development of strategy cannot be broken down so simply into discrete steps within such a meeting structure. The thinking evolves: strategic analysis ideas are tried out to help inform and stimulate discussion, people attempt to make sense of a situation both individually and collectively, there is intensity to the mental energy and depth of communication involved. Meetings can finish without clear conclusions or without the completion of a defined stage of the work; only partial progress might have been made in reaching satisfactory answers to the questions posed, with people still trying to develop a shared understanding or work through the implications. They might be struggling to make sense of a particular element of this, or perhaps the conversation is flowing and they are making good progress but just have run out of time. Dispersing back to their respective job locations, with the immediate demands of their operational responsibilities, the lists of actions and the need to switch their attention to other meetings and inputs, they will quickly lose the momentum of thinking that had been developed during their strategising; when they next convene they will need to spend time and energy tuning in again and re-engaging their collective thinking.

Developing a 'working document' that captures the thinking will help this continuity. Meeting minutes in the usual style are unlikely to be effective in this, and transcribing flipchart notes can record the points made but might not show how these fit into the flow of thinking and discussion. A working document aims to articulate this thinking, both to capture the progress that has been made and also – importantly – to act as a platform for the next discussion.

The work involved in developing such a document is itself part of the strategising process. It is much more than just a record of the previous discussion. Instead, its aim is to summarise, clarify and articulate where the thinking has reached. Drafting such a working document means making sense of the discussion, finding an effective way to convey the key ideas which those involved will recognise but without necessarily repeating all the detailed steps involved in getting there. However, it does require revisiting the thinking, putting each point discussed in a context, grouping the topics so people can recognise how they fit. It is also an opportunity to stimulate further thinking. In the process of developing this, questions might occur which need clarification – an implicit assumption not tested, a stated fact which needs evidence, perhaps even an apparent flaw in the logic. And some of the questions to be explored during the next discussion opportunity might become apparent; drafting the working document requires tuning in again to the thinking in the previous meeting, trying to articulate this can prompt questions and the momentum of the thought flow can carry forward into identifying what needs to be considered next.

This working document can be used both as a summary of the thinking developed during each discussion and a platform for the next; it can be revised and updated – or rewritten – after each such discussion. Often it might not have captured this in a way that works for everyone – points might have been misinterpreted, the way in which ideas are articulated might not resonate with people's thinking; maybe the way in which the argument is developed does not fit with their preferred logic flow (for example, for some people working through the argument step by step to build up to the conclusion helps them understand the rationale, whereas others might prefer to start with the summary and refer subsequently to the supporting steps). However, its aim is to provide a basis for such discussion, an attempt to articulate the thinking in a way that those involved can relate to – and if a draft prompts conversations that lead to a clearer shared understanding, then it is serving its purpose.

The drafting and redrafting of such a working document to reflect developing thinking is a key content tool to help the strategy journey, acting as a reference point and providing continuity to the process. This iterative approach, continually restating and refining the crucial strategy rationale, helps clarify and sharpen how this is articulated, both as a reference for those directly involved and also as a vehicle to share the thinking more widely. It does need to be understood and accepted that this document reflects the work in progress, and not a definitive conclusion to it; it is not wrong to not get it right first time! At the same time it can be used (adapted as appropriate) to help share the developing thinking and check it for sense, for example feeding in ideas to other workstreams, updating others interested, clarifying any issues or concerns and ensuring there is consistency and fit within any wider organisational strategy context.

A strategy journey is a voyage of exploration for an organisation, to chart new territory and decide on the paths to be taken. A working document as we have described captures the current thinking of those who are finding the paths; it is their latest 'view from here', how they see the way ahead, to be refined and improved as further steps are taken and more is learnt.

Radical inquisition

Strategies can look good and sound grand. Sophistication can be impressive; who can fail to admire the cleverness behind a succinctly presented idea or applaud the ambition of a motivating vision? Especially when one appreciates just how much effort has gone into crafting these and how the achievement is lauded by those with influence in the organisation.

Whose, then, will be the quiet voice at the strategy emperor's parade that says, 'I don't understand!'?

Such an intervention so late in the process is of course not ideal, so it is important to ensure there is constructive critical challenge as an integral part of the strategy formulation process. (The emphasis here is on constructive; there is a common objective, to develop the best strategy for the organisation, which needs to override any individual perspectives or political positioning.)

Developing strategy is as much of an art as a science. Strategy is crafted from an interpretation of relationships: the relationship of people in the organisation and how they perceive its purpose and values and culture; its relationships with its customers and users of its products or services and with other stakeholders with a strong interest vested in the organisation; and the relationship of the organisation to others serving the same people, operating in the same market 'space'. Forming a picture, a clear, shared view about these relationships, is the foundation from which the organisation develops its strategy. That picture – its clarity, sharpness and credibility – is therefore crucial.

So, does this picture make sense? How credible is the analysis from which it was derived? Does it feel right, does it ring true?

The use of these terms, mirroring NLP sensory channel preferences, is deliberate. As well as the robustness of the rationale – is the logic sound? Are the assumptions upon which it is based reasonable? It is also worth taking notice of one's 'gut instincts'. There are instances where despite the apparent incontestability of the logic, there can be an inner 'nagging doubt' that something has been missed, that there is an illogical flaw in what has been developed. Such instincts ought not to be ignored, but should prompt a re-examination of the rationale by which this view of the organisation has been developed. They might be allayed or reinforced; the important point is to test both the logic and the intuition.

When we are dealing with something familiar we tend to get caught up in the accepted framework for considering it: the terminology, the established ways of looking at situations, the anecdotes that influence perceptions. Challenging this framework, this organisation view, can be difficult – yet an effective strategy development process will test this. Using our journey analogy, consider planning to set out using a map and compass because 'that's what we've always used and it's worked for us', rather than adopting GPS technology, for example.

Constructive robustness

Three examples to illustrate the importance of challenging firmly:

1   When people are working intensely on a subject, giving it their full focus and becoming engrossed in its intricate details, it is easy to assume that everyone else is as familiar with the topic and can quickly tune in to the same wavelength of thinking. In the enthusiasm to communicate the outcome of their work the terminology used might presume a level of understanding that overestimates the audience's familiarity, and the explanation might 'jump' some steps in the argument that might appear obvious to those working on it but that are essential 'links' the audience must make to understand the rationale fully. Whilst people might have the utmost confidence in the knowledge and abilities of the working group, each person has to work through the same logic steps for themselves to confirm the conclusions; the skill in presenting the argument is to not short-cut these key steps, but to make them clear and succinct to make it easy for each person in the audience to come to the same conclusions quickly and efficiently. Going through this process is important if people are to understand the subject and feel confident about accepting the argument; asking 'Do I really understand this?' and probing accordingly is a valid challenge that in no way signifies a lack of trust in those who have worked on it, but rather is a constructive step to help make the rationale more accessible.

2   In developing an argument it is often useful to consider how that argument might work from others' perspectives. Indeed, approaching the subject in this way can help strengthen the rationale. The rationale for a particular strategic initiative might seem compelling from the point of view of those involved in its development but may be less relevant or convincing to others. Deliberately wearing others' hats (metaphorically speaking!) and approaching the argument from their perspective can help identify what might be important or relevant to them, and addressing this can strengthen the overall justification or prompt consideration of the implications for how others might respond.

As an example, a provider of commissioned services in a regulated sector might be developing a strategic initiative to expand its geographical area of operation, based on its proven success elsewhere and superior capabilities – a strong case from its own perspective. However, when considered from a commissioner's perspective this could be seen as putting pressure on stretched budgets and destabilising other providers who also provide different services; recognising these as likely concerns and considering how to address them will lead to a more robust assessment of the strategic initiative and an approach that is more likely to succeed. (In this example, realising that the provider would need to demonstrate how overall improved outcomes and more cost-effective use of the commissioner's budget would be achieved, whilst not jeopardising the sustainability of other services, could alter how the organisation develops its strategic initiative.

3   Sometimes the strategy that is being proposed is simply wrong, and a robust (but constructive) challenge is needed at the strategy development stage to avoid potential failure. An example from my personal experience:

GrandMet Brewing was one of the UK's major drinks companies in the 1980s, responsible for the brewing, sales and distribution in the UK of international brands like Carlsberg, Foster's, Holsten and Budweiser, as well as a range of British beers. The marketing strategy included heavy investment in advertising these brands, plus a programme of promotions for the individual brands that the sales force were tasked to persuade their licensed on-trade customers to run in their bars, pubs and clubs. However, take-up was very low (although if the promotions contained branded merchandise such as T-shirts then the promotional kits would all be distributed, although evidence of the promotions being run in bars was sparse). Clearly this strategy was both ineffective and wasteful. The inclination of some was to criticise the sales force for failing to obtain their customers' commitment, and tighter monitoring of sales force performance was recommended to strengthen implementation of the strategy.

After talking to salespeople, it soon became apparent that bar owners found these promotions to be of little value (although the T-shirts were useful!); they required a lot of effort to set up but simply encouraged their customers to switch brands rather than increase the total amount they spent at the bar. Whilst in the short term this met the objectives of the marketing team to promote sales of the individual brands, there was no longer-term change in people's preferences for which beers they drank. So, a significant amount of money was being spent on promotional kits perceived by bar owners to be of no benefit to *their* businesses, and the sales force was being pushed to expend even more effort every month to ensure the kits were used.

What followed was a debate within the organisation which challenged the current strategy, informed by evidence from salespeople and customers and by looking at the situation from the perspective of the bar owners as well as the objectives of the organisation. The result was the development of a revised strategy that took into account customers' needs, not just for brand promotions, but ultimately for how GrandMet Brewing sought to increase sales of the brands in its portfolio and consequently how it organised its sales force. Brand-themed promotions were developed which aimed to increase total bar takings as well as sales of the brand, targeted at specific types of bars, with more thought given to making them easy to run in a busy pub; different strategies were developed for increasing sales according to defined criteria, and sales force priorities were articulated more clearly, with measures and rewards structured accordingly.

It would have been very easy in the prior example to accept the current thinking and not challenge it, but the strategy relied on a view of what was happening that was incorrect – and when evidence began to emerge that brought it into question, it was clear that further investigation was necessary, as well as a re-examining of the established model upon which the strategy was based. Earlier in this chapter I used the example of United Biscuits and how consumer research led to a new way of looking at market segmentation as an illustration of the value of insights; what I did not mention was that this also prompted extensive strategic debate within the company, including challenging the conclusions developed by a high-profile management consultancy that was working with the senior management of the company at that time.

Strategy is important: developing the right strategy is vitally important. It should be based on sound logic developed from robust assumptions, reviewed critically but constructively and tested from different perspectives; challenge has a crucial role in the development of an effective strategic plan.

What if?

We have seen how powerful questions and questioning can be in developing effective strategic plans. In this next section we will look at three ways in which one simple question can be very useful.

The science of hypothesis

Our consideration of the future is predicated on assumptions: 'If things carry on like this, then . . .'; 'If X does Y, then I'll do Z'; 'We're planning a holiday in July when it is likely to be good weather' – and so on. Strategies are also based on assumptions that an organisation's assessment of its current situation and the factors likely to affect it are reasonably accurate. Yet it is an implicit 'If' that precedes this statement; we have to make decisions based on our best assessment of a situation and judge how likely we think it is that the assessment will turn out to be realistic.

'What if . . .?' is a key phrase in formulating strategies. Strategies are developed based on a model that is assumed to be accurate, that people have developed as a shared view of where the organisation is now and what might affect its future. For example, a technology company might have reached the view based on a couple of recent successes that one of its core competencies is its ability to take emerging technologies from small research and development companies and work out how to scale these up to commercial manufacturing levels; during its strategic planning it is considering what its strategy might be based on this assessment. This might involve focusing on this as a differentiating competency, building up its capabilities by recruiting suitably skilled technicians and engineers, extending this capability to other sectors or a targeted acquisition programme to obtain the intellectual property rather than just license the technologies. These various strategies were based on their initial assessment of their strengths and how these compare to similar companies in the same field. They have asked the question, 'If this is the case, how might we consider taking advantage of it?'

They will then go through a process of evaluating these various strategies. Each one needs to be thought through, together with its possible implications; for example:

- 'If we adopt this strategy, what might happen?'
- 'Should we focus only on this?'
- 'What will we need to do as a company? How will we change?'
- 'What will this mean for other areas in our business? Do we continue with them or divest?'
- 'How might other companies in our field respond?'

So there is a series of questions that are prompted by asking, 'What if we adopt this strategy?' Equally important is to ask 'What if we don't adopt this strategy?' leading to a similar series of questions.

Considering the possible implications of a strategy also involves 'What if . . .?' questions. The last example in the prior list can lead to some interesting options as people start to think through the situation from the point of view of each competitor; wearing a 'different hat' can stimulate some creative thinking, which might be significant in deciding whether to adopt this strategy. Whilst focusing on what is perceived to be a differentiating competency might seem to be an exciting strategic opportunity, if this could be easily countered by a competitor's strategy (for example, using their financial balance sheet strength to negotiate licensing deals for the most promising emerging technologies), then this strategy might carry a greater long-term financial risk.

There is also a 'What if . . .?' question at the root of the strategy deliberations. These have been developed from an assessment of the organisations' current situation, but this assessment might not be accurate. What if, for example, the success of our technology company in scaling up emerging technologies on those two occasions was due to factors other than the technical and engineering expertise in the company? Perhaps it was a particular aspect of the technology or involved materials that one of the engineers had studied in her PhD research; recognising that the initial assessment from which the thinking developed might not be accurate is a pivotal step.

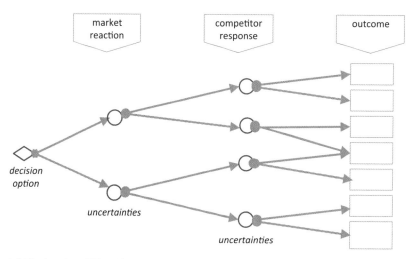

Figure 6.5 Evaluating 'What if . . .?'

We all prefer certainty. And there has to be belief in the thinking that goes into developing a strategic plan and the confidence that it will result in strengthening the organisation's ability to get to where it wants to be. But appreciating that a strategic plan is based on a set of assumptions – albeit ones that have been selected using the organisation's best judgement – and that the thinking is based on these is a healthy perspective that can influence an organisation's approach to strategic planning. Compare these two alternative models of a strategic plan:

1 A comprehensive document that sets out ambitious targets for the organisation, defines clear strategies for each key function and maps out detailed plans and projections by departments for the next five years, together with key performance indicators by which the board will track progress quarterly.
2 A document that summarises and reminds people of what they want their organisation to aim for and the principles and strategies they have developed to help them achieve this, together with the reasoning they used in developing these, giving them the confidence to be able to respond to changes from the initial assumptions.

Neither is necessarily 'better', but in a fast-changing environment the ability to adapt is likely to be a desirable attribute, and the better the understanding across the organisation of how their strategy was developed from their initial assessment of the organisation's situation, the greater the capability of the organisation to respond to changes.

The art of projections

Projections are the vital link between strategies and plans; in our journey analogy we consider first which path we should take, and how to tackle the terrain we expect to encounter, and then we work out how far we think we will travel each day, what equipment we will need and what supplies we require. We might

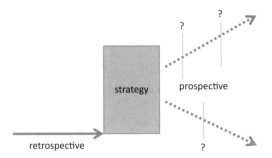

Figure 6.6 Projections perspectives

consider several different paths which all look likely options, but in projecting the requirements we could come to the conclusion that some are more feasible than others. Similarly with strategic planning; we need to develop projections to help us evaluate various strategic options, as well as to form the basis of our plan for the option we choose.

Projections are based on assumptions, and it is the transparency of those assumptions that is key to using them effectively. This applies both to the information that is used as inputs and the method by which the projections are developed. Having a clear, consistent set of assumptions and understanding the model that is used are both important. People need to be able to follow the logic of how projections are derived so that if the assumptions change, or a more accurate way of modelling is developed, revised projections can be produced.

Developing a projection model can be challenging: the available data might not be ideal, and how this relates to the outputs required might not be apparent, so assumptions need to be made using best judgement. Approximations might have to suffice for imperfect data. Unintentional inaccuracies might abound – but the important point is that they will be visible so that they can be changed when better information becomes available. But it is worth investing the effort to develop as good a model as can be achieved with the information and knowledge available.

It is also valid to reflect the uncertainty of projections by using a range rather than a single number output. Like any forecasts, the only certainty is that the projections will not be precisely accurate. Ranges can help with maximum/minimum and best case/worst case projections.

A questioning approach can help develop a good model. Projections can be an aspect of strategic planning some people can struggle with, and often an initial attempt is based simply on extrapolating historic data. But it is also necessary to explore the context for this and the factors that might affect it. For example, consider the questions that might be asked when developing projections for sales of Brand X via a single channel in a single geographical territory market:

- What have been the sales of X historically? Is the rate of change year on year (e.g., annual per cent growth or decline) increasing or decreasing?
- Do we know of any factors that have influenced this (for example, was there a change of pricing strategy or a change in distribution)?

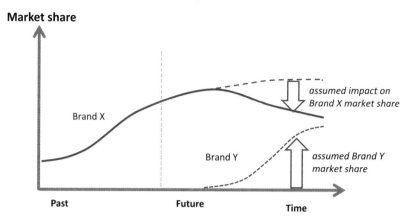

Figure 6.7 Projection model

- What is the market context for this? What has been its annual rate of growth or decline? Do we know of any factors that have contributed to this?
- How have the market shares of X and its competitors changed over this period? Were there new entrants to the market which altered the market share mix?

Already this is building up a richer picture about what might have influenced Brand X's sales over this period and helping us identify some of the factors that might affect our projections. We might know of possible future developments that we need to build into the projection model. For example, a competitor new product launch might be expected, and we will need to make a 'best judgement' estimate of its potential impact. Maybe this can be quantified in an estimate of actual sales, or perhaps an assumption can be made about what market share it might take over time and if it will increase the total size of the market or just take share from all the other products in the market, either proportionate to their current shares or affecting some brands disproportionately.

We can see from this simple example that there is quite an art to developing a projection model, and each of the questions will lead to a stated assumption. This transparency of assumptions and method enables the model to be dynamic – when assumptions change, it becomes easy to revise the projections, and also to update them in future years.

Projection models are also key in organising how to implement the strategic plan, linking activity to facilities to resources and the financial plan. The same approach applies to developing projections for the numbers and skill mix of people who will be needed for sales or activity volumes, for example; the assumptions and methods of calculation need to be transparent and clearly explained. Narrative is important, highlighting the factors influencing these and any implications. For example, the intended strategy might require a significant increase in the number of people with a particular skill that is in short supply, leading to early recruitment initiatives as part of the plan and perhaps identifying this as one of the risks that could affect achievement of the projections.

Developing linked, dynamic, transparent projection models covering all key aspects of the organisation – activity/sales, capacity/facilities, resources/people, finances and any others or subsets relevant to that organisation – helps consideration of the implications, dependencies and risks involved in implementing a particular strategy. Operating to a consistent set of assumptions, different options or variations of an option can be modelled to develop a suite of projections; the strategic plan can be 'stress tested' to assess what might happen if some of the variables changed.

Working through the implications can highlight risks or result in changes to the plan. Using the earlier illustration as an example, halving the original assumption of share loss to a competitor might result in a projected increase in sales of 5 per cent, which would mean bringing forward by a year the need to invest in additional manufacturing capacity. This has implications for workforce numbers both in the factory and the sales force; given the shortage of engineers the company cannot rely on recruiting these in time, but reducing its turnover of engineers (which is high given the market demand) as well as recruiting might enable it to meet the projected requirement. Consequently an improved rewards and career development strategy for engineers would need to be considered in this scenario. However, the increased cost of the revised remuneration strategy (taking into account the need to adjust this for related groups also) would reduce net contribution levels from 35 per cent of total sales value to 33 per cent for three years until production efficiencies in the new manufacturing plant started to be achieved.

This fictional example illustrates the power of such a suite of linked projection models. It enables people to consider what might happen if some of the assumptions change, and – importantly – it stimulates and informs conversations about this as a key part of the development of the strategic plan. This can help identify risks as well as implications and is an essential step in evaluating different strategic options.

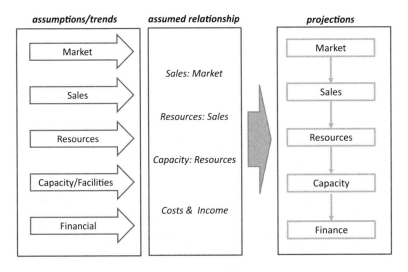

Figure 6.8 Linked projection model

A consideration of scenarios

Developing strategy involves new insights, fresh ways of looking at a situation and creative thinking, combining an open-minded search for answers with thorough logic and constructive challenge to make sense of where the organisation should aim to go. The type of thinking and conversations this requires are different from those usually associated with the more operational transactions in the day-to-day work of an organisation, and as we have noted previously it can be hard for people to switch to this mindset, requiring time to 'tune in' to a different pace and depth of thought. It requires disconnecting from the immediate issues and tasks to contemplate the longer term and stepping back to consider the bigger picture: to be able to think through the implications and the implications of the implications, yet in a hypothetical 'What if?' way. And then it requires judgement, to make choices and decisions that might or might not prove the right ones, but that will have a major impact on the organisation's future.

Thinking through scenarios is an excellent way to develop this thinking and open the mind to different possibilities. It is also a powerful technique to engage other stakeholders; those participating in scenario planning will have a shared understanding of the thinking and a shared view of how the future could be, providing a common reference point to which subsequent conversations can return.

Scenarios are based on asking 'What if . . .?' – persistently, rigorously and thoroughly. Different situations, different options, different possible futures can be explored collectively by considering a set of assumptions and thinking through what the consequences and implications might be. This can be especially useful early in the strategising phase, as the following fictional example will help illustrate:

> It is early 2018. Hospital K, a large teaching hospital with strong research links to the local university, is in the early stages of developing a new strategic plan. The National Health Service (NHS) in England is at a pivotal point; the previous two winters saw hospitals struggling to cope with cancelled operations and long waiting lists, and public opinion is divided between those who think it is a failed model and those who attribute its problems to underfunding. The next UK General Election is two years away, and the future of the NHS is set to be one of the major issues debated; yet further 'reform' to the system seems inevitable, but no-one can be certain what form this will take.
>
> As part of considering 'Where are we now?' the senior team assessed what they believed to be the key political, economic, social and technological (PEST) factors affecting themselves and the wider NHS and realised that the significant uncertainty meant that they had two options: they could either develop a strategic plan based on the current NHS model and then react to whatever changes might be introduced after the General Election, or they could think through what some of those changes might be and – whilst they would not turn out exactly as they had assumed – at least they would be prepared in their thinking to be able to make strategic decisions once the new government was elected and started to show its intentions.
>
> There were two phases to this work, both involving intense, focused workshops that included both senior managers and clinical leaders, facilitated by

people skilled in strategic foresight and developing scenarios. During the first phase they discussed the factors identified in their PEST analysis and worked through which they thought were most significant, and they subsequently developed four scenarios which would enable them to explore these further and develop their thinking about what the implications might be for their hospital:

A   *Regional planning*

In this scenario a new organisation is set up in each region in England to plan and manage all the healthcare needs of the population. Modelled on the Swedish healthcare system, these regional health authorities will commission providers of healthcare services to be responsible for specific types of care. In some cases this might be by planning and coordinating services across existing hospitals (some will stop providing services duplicated with other hospitals; other regions are likely to invite any providers – whether NHS or not – to tender for newly defined 'packages of services').

B   *Local integration*

The health needs of the local population are intricately bound up with people's well-being and lifestyles, and in this scenario an expert organisation is set up responsible to the local council to achieve improvements, including public health initiatives (e.g., related to reducing smoking and alcohol-related illnesses and social costs, nutrition and exercise, housing conditions, mental health, elderly care and so on), as well as manage the general practitioners and hospitals who treat ill health. As well as tackling the causes of ill health, this system aims to provide better care for people due to leave hospital, thereby reducing patients' time in hospital and making more beds available to care for more people (or faster).

C   *System innovation*

This scenario assumes that the new government has realised that top-down changes to the healthcare system usually result in organisations learning how to play to the new rules, rather than responding to the principles intended by the system reforms. This scenario assumes that they free up the central controls to encourage healthcare organisations to think creatively and form partnerships and collaborations to develop innovative ways of addressing healthcare needs, whether locally or nationally. It is an open door to consider radical solutions, but developed by those with the front-line knowledge and skills to try to make these work.

D   *Independent in a part-privatised system*

In this scenario the NHS is opened up fully to private providers, and patients are required to pay for some treatments deemed 'non-essential' as a way of rationing the available budget. The organisations commissioning healthcare services, previously part of the NHS, have been given semi-independent status – an initial step, some think, to the United States model of accountable care organisations who 'buy' healthcare services for the people they represent (whether through geography or on behalf of healthcare insurers).

These are 'rich' scenarios, vividly painted pictures of hypothetical situations that help people think themselves into each scene and imagine the organisation in that position. Collectively, there is a common platform for people to discuss the implications for the organisation and the options open to it for responding. This is the second phase of the work. The intensity of the thinking and discussing might require some time to allow people to work through the issues. There are also questions about the organisation's purpose, values and principles that these scenarios might unearth, and these need to be discussed and debated. Thinking through these scenarios will ensure these are made explicit and identified as issues that need to be resolved. Had the organisation chosen the other option of developing its strategic plan based only on the current system, not only would it have been faced with the need to think through its responses reactively, but these deeper, more fundamental issues would have had to be tackled then as part of this. Instead, by undertaking this scenario planning exercise, the organisation can address these issues prior to the need to make choices. In addition, it has thought through what its strategic responses might be and is able to start preparing for them.

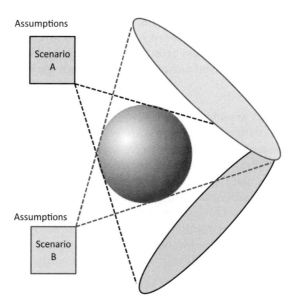

Figure 6.9 Scenarios

Organisational performance = $f(x_i, \theta_j)$

where

x_i = factors outside organisation's control

θ_j = factors within organisation's control

Figure 6.10 Organisational performance

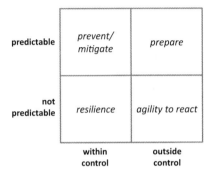

Figure 6.11 Predictable-control grid

However prepared an organisation is for what might happen in the future, however clear its strategy and thorough its planning, much can happen to affect what actually occurs. Some of this might have been anticipated; other possibilities will not have been foreseen. Markets are not deterministic constructs operating to predictable rules, but the flux of a host of players acting and interacting in the same space; organisations are not just structures of defined roles and processes as much as a collection of people engaged in the same endeavour.

What happens to an organisation is a combination of events or developments under its control and external factors that it can't influence.

Assessing and managing risks is an important element in developing a strategic plan, despite sometimes being considered only an afterthought to the effort and energy focused on producing a strategic plan document. Considering the risks should be an integral part of the strategy journey (the analogy with a real journey is very obvious!); it enables the organisation to deal with the risks it can control and strengthens its ability to cope with those it can't.

Identifying risks is all about asking 'What if . . .?' and following through the implications. As is the case when developing scenarios, this requires both creative thinking and logic, considering the possibilities for what might happen and then mentally imagining the organisation in that situation and thinking through the likely consequences. It might help to think of this as a three-stage process:

1   The first step is to think about what types of risks there might be that could affect the organisation when implementing its strategic plan. For example, there are risks arising from the organisation's own capabilities and those from external factors; the former might include physical aspects (e.g., capacity, production), people (skills, leadership) and processes (e.g., information systems), and the latter could comprise factors such as market (consumer trends, competitors), regulatory (e.g., compliance issues) and political (in the case of Hospital K earlier in this chapter). The categories developed will be those that are useful for the organisation. Once again this is about shared meaning, developing a framework that helps people in the organisation understand the various types of risks.

2   The next step is to think of all the risks that might occur within each category. This could become an exhaustive and encyclopaedic exercise, covering all possible eventualities. But focusing on those risks that are either likely to occur or that could have a significant impact on the organisation will help keep this manageable. It makes sense to group or consolidate some of these into areas or themes, although in summarising them in this way it is important to avoid losing some of the specific individual risks and the thinking that has gone into them.

There might also be a tendency to consider levels upon levels of risks. For example, not identifying and dealing with risks effectively is also a risk, which, whilst strictly logical, could divert attention from more significant practical risks.

3   Assessing the likelihood and impact of each risk helps give a sense of proportion to the various risks. Using a tool like the risk assessment grid illustrated earlier in this chapter (Figure 6.4) is useful in conveying this pictorially.

4   The final step is to discuss and agree upon what the organisation should do in the event of each risk happening and what steps it can take – preventatively or reactively – to mitigate the risk, either reducing the impact or reducing the likelihood.

Category	Risks		Risk assessment		Mitigating likelihood		Mitigating impact	
Type of risk	Risk	What if . . . ?	Likelihood	Impact	Action	Reduced likelihood	Action	Reduced impact
A	A1	X	High	Medium		Medium		-
	A2	Y	Low	High		-		Medium
		Z	Medium	Low		-		-
B	B1		etc					
	B2							
C	C1							
D	D1							
	D2							

Figure 6.12 Assessing risks

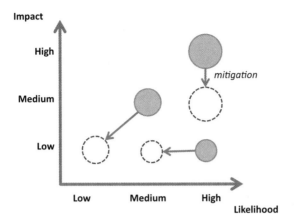

Figure 6.13 Risk mitigation

In this chapter we have considered some of the content that helps in developing a strategic plan: the value of insights, using pictures and grids to communicate information effectively, how iteration and working documents help in developing the thinking and the importance of robust but constructive challenge. We also discussed the power of asking, 'What if . . .?' and how it can be used in developing projections, considering scenarios and assessing risks.

In the next chapter we will discuss how to bring all this together.

7

THE STORY

How do you capture the results of all the thinking and conversations that have occurred during the process of developing a strategic plan and summarise the outcome of the strategising and organising undertaken on the strategy journey?

A question often asked early in a strategic planning process is what the completed strategic plan document will look like – what the key sections will be, how it will be structured, if there will be other supporting documents or appendices including more detailed information. For some people it helps to have an idea of the end product, to know what they are aiming to achieve; others perhaps perceive the process as providing the words and numbers for predefined sections, ticking off each as it is completed.

Such a question assumes a focus on the strategic plan document rather than the broader perspective of the three dimensions of strategic planning, *context*, *process* and *content*. In our journey analogy it is like trying to define at the outset what will be recorded about the adventure on which people are about to embark. Yet this can help people approach the strategic planning process with a better understanding and more confidence, so how do we respond to the question?

Let us return to the four questions that a strategy journey aims to address:

1   *Where are we now?*
2   *Where do we want to go?*
3   *How do we get there?*
4   *How do we make it happen?*

In essence, the purpose of a strategic plan document is to record the answers to these, so a working framework can be based on this to help understanding. We could explain a little more about each question to help further, described in ways appropriate to the organisation, and develop an outline that in effect is a guide to answering the questions. A generic example might look something like this (excluding an executive summary and any appendices containing more detailed supporting information):

A   The context: why we have developed this strategic plan
B   Our current situation (*Where are we now?*):

    a   Our market – how it has developed, key factors and current trends
    b   Our competitors – their position in the market, strengths and weaknesses
    c   Our organisation

- Where we fit in the market, our key relationships, how others perceive us
- Our key competencies: what we are good at, where we need to improve
- What are our key opportunities, and what do we think are the major threats?

C   Our objectives and strategic direction (*Where do we want to go?*):

a   What we think might happen in the future (scenarios)
b   Our options and how we have evaluated them
c   Our strategic objectives/chosen strategy/vision for the future

D   Our plan to achieve this (*How do we get there?*)

a   Strategic initiatives: how we need to change/what we need to do to be able to achieve our objectives/our priorities for investment (time/energy/money)
b   What resources will we need, and how will we organise them?
c   Our sales/capacity/resources/financial projections

E   Implementing the strategy (*How do we make it happen?*)

a   What are the risks to our plan, and how will we address these?
b   How will we measure our progress/ensure we are on track?
c   How will we ensure we can adapt if things change?

Whilst this is a reasonably general outline and a logical approach, it lacks the specific organisational context. Also influencing this will be the reasons the organisation is developing a strategic plan at this time and the analysis of who is interested and hence who are the primary intended audiences. It needs more specific questions, more relevance to the organisation and a more engaging style if it is to 'come to life' as a powerful and motivating distillation of the organisation's strategy journey. Let us look at some ways of approaching this that might help.

Throughout this book we have seen how questions are a powerful driver of the strategic planning process, from the four questions that map out the stages on the journey to the more specific questions that develop from these. The organisation's strategic plan is developed by answering these questions; the strategic plan document articulates these answers, weaving them together in a narrative that makes sense for the organisation. A good story is engaging and memorable; it is accessible and easily understood; and it can stimulate more thoughts, ideas and actions.

So how might we help bring the strategic plan story to life?

Words and pictures

In the last chapter we discussed how 2-D representations – diagrams, grids, tables – can help convey ideas more simply and effectively than trying to express them in text. Drawing pictures and mapping connections and flows are part of the dynamics of the rich conversations that occur in answering the questions, making sense of a situation and developing a shared understanding. Including the most helpful of these visual representations in the strategic plan document will help communicate that meaning, reflecting the thinking that was involved.

Fascinatingly, in every strategic planning process I have experienced there seems to be one particular diagram or grid that was pivotal in helping people express a key idea at a crucial stage of the strategising. This picture becomes a constant reference point for the subsequent thinking, remaining unchanged in every iteration and featuring prominently in the strategic plan document.

The advantages of 2-D in helping people understand key points applies also when considering what format a strategic plan document should adopt (assuming of course that this has not been stipulated externally). The aim of the document is to summarise the answers to questions succinctly and enable them to be understood easily. Communicating a complex or multifaceted line of reasoning with supporting information can be made much easier using a 2-D 'canvas'. In a traditional written report format, where the reader follows the argument line by line (like reading a book), it is difficult to see the relationship between the different parts of the argument; this requires much scrolling up and down the page (or between pages), moving back and forth between paragraphs, with the risk of losing the flow or the relationship between the parts.

Imaging the page as a canvas on which to express just one topic, or a self-contained part of the argument, allows the freedom to adopt a 2-D approach, designing the layout to communicate the flow of the argument and the relationship between the various parts of this.

The two ideas in this approach, that first of trying to communicate a single topic or argument on one page and second in considering that page to be a canvas on which one can express this, encourage viewing the drafting of a strategic plan document as a creative challenge, with the objective of communicating the content succinctly and effectively.

Of course, this might not suit every organisation. The format for the strategic plan document might be predefined, and the preference of those in the organisation who are ultimately responsible for the strategic plan might be for a more 'traditional' approach. Indeed, when I first used the '2-D canvas' approach in helping an organisation prepare its strategic plan document there was some scepticism and raised eyebrows until people saw a draft and realised the advantages of this format.

The selection of software tools to compile the document is obviously one for each organisation to consider. Word processing programmes are the usual choice for the traditional 1-D written report format, but they can have limited functionality to

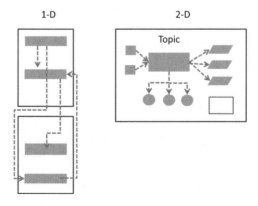

Figure 7.1 Argument flows

position objects on the page in 2-D. Presentation or publication software might have more flexibility for this (although of course in the case of presentation software it is being used as a document editor rather than to develop slides for presentation). The use of 'slide decks' for reports is becoming more common, where slides are used as pages for reading rather than presentation; the popularity of infographics illustrates the appeal of communicating information using a combination of visuals and text, designing the layout to show the relationship between the elements on the page.

Themes

There is much to communicate in a strategic plan. Whilst the questions that led the process through its four stages were simple, the answers are more complex. Communicating these involves explaining the background, helping people understand the most pertinent information and taking them through the rationale for the choices that have been made and decisions taken, explaining the thinking in a succinct and focused way so they can understand how these conclusions have been derived.

The generic document structure used as an example earlier in this chapter adopts a logical step-by-step approach following the four stages; it takes an organisation-wide scope at each stage. However, as the thinking develops during an organisation's strategy journey several areas of particular focus can emerge, issues that are common to various workstreams, aspects of the organisation that need sustained concerted effort to improve, maybe the need to change the culture of the organisation. In working out, "How do we get there?" it makes sense to focus on these areas, to organise working groups to concentrate on addressing this for each area. Two examples to help illustrate this:

1   Workgroups were set up in Company X to assess the current situation from sales, marketing, logistics, manufacturing and finance perspectives. In their analyses:

   - The sales workgroup identified customer dissatisfaction with frequent out-of-stock delays in fulfilling orders for some products
   - The marketing group was concerned about declining market share for these brands
   - Inaccurate forecasting was highlighted by the logistics workgroup as a key issue
   - The manufacturing group felt that production scheduling could be more efficient
   - The additional costs of not fulfilling orders in full was one of the 'opportunities for improvement' flagged by the finance workgroup.

   The common thread running through these was a weakness in the organisation's ability to meet demand for its products. Although each of the workgroups had highlighted a particular problem area, it was clear when considered overall that there was no single area that was the root of the problem, rather that it was a system issue – from forecasting to production scheduling – that needed to be addressed, and this became one of the company-wide strategic initiatives in the organisation's strategic plan.

2   In chapter 4 we used the example of entrepreneurial technology start-up D which had grown over five years and was now spread over several sites, with variations in working practices and remuneration structures. D had embarked on developing a strategic plan to help decide on a strategy for the next phase of its growth, and initially the strategising focused on considering various technologies and market opportunities and its competences and capabilities. However, in the discussions amongst the teams across the company there was some grumbling about perceived preferential treatment for people at other sites. Probing further, it became apparent that this was not just about pay and job structures, but also about how decisions were taken, different styles of management and how important people felt each site was within the organisation. It was clear that the company needed to work on its values and culture and establish common practices that would demonstrate fairness and consistency across all locations and staff groups. This became one of the themes in its strategic plan, titled 'One Company' but involving initiatives on company structure, rewards and career progression and developing a values-based culture. The company's strategic plan included two other themes as well, about its strategy for growth (and how it would decide about future opportunities) and consolidating its infrastructure to underpin the organisation's expansion.

Identifying strategic themes that group together various elements from the strategic planning process helps provide focus for the organisation and gives a framework for implementing initiatives that address these elements. They are part of the story of the organisation's strategy journey. Focusing on a small number of themes rather than a long list of projects and actions helps keep the story simple and memorable. As we will see in part 3, one of the characteristics of an effective strategic plan is how people in the organisation can refer to it and use it as a platform for decisions and actions over the duration of the plan, and not just in the months immediately following the conclusion of that strategy journey. A simple, focused and easy-to-remember story that makes sense to people and helps them understand where the organisation is heading is more likely to achieve this.

Identifying specific challenges is also a useful way of focusing attention on implementation and action. Strategic themes could themselves be presented as challenges. Or, given that a strategic plan is intended to provide direction for the organisation over the longer term, it might be appropriate to focus on the current specific challenges (or challenge) within each theme. This approach enables the challenges to be updated later in the life of the strategic plan, with the theme providing continuity of the strategy whilst focusing on the new challenge will re-energise the implementation.

Strategies are about organisations; although the organisation might be structured into functions or departments, it is the whole organisation that undertakes a strategy journey. Strategic initiatives require implementation across the organisation; explaining the role that each team in the organisation can play in this is a key part of the detail of answering, "How do we get there?" It is important too that everyone at all levels of the organisation understands the rationale for a strategic initiative, how it fits within and contributes to the organisation's overall strategy, and not just their department's or job function's part in this. Themes are a useful way of providing a framework that helps people make sense of this, and themes act as a powerful way of referring back to the strategic plan. A project is about organising resources and tasks; a strategic

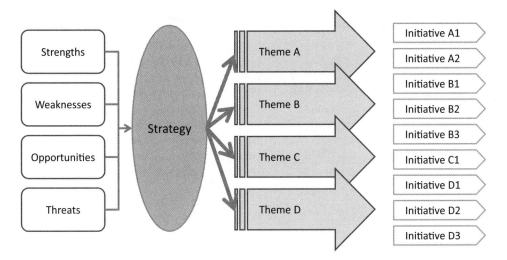

Figure 7.2 Developing the themes

initiative is about the organisation achieving a specific goal or direction; and a theme within the strategic plan is about people understanding why. When projects encounter problems, when timetables slip or a project struggles to deliver the expected benefits, people can consider other ways of still implementing the strategic initiative; similarly when there are difficulties in progressing a strategic initiative, understanding the overall purpose and intent behind it will help the organisation continue to strive to achieve it despite a setback affecting one particular element.

Making sense

Although producing a strategic plan document is only one element of developing a strategic plan, capturing the organisation's strategy journey in a way that it can use to help it reach its intended goals is an important task in that journey. Whilst the strategic planning process, the rich conversations, the choices and decisions and the content generated along the way have all contributed to the strategy journey, this is an opportunity to articulate the story in a way that people can use as a common reference and platform to help them make decisions and adapt to future changes.

This is a creative process involving crafting the strategy story to bring it to life, explaining the thinking, highlighting the strategic objectives and the themes and initiatives by which they might be achieved, making it accessible and understandable. Just as there might be advantages in a 2-D canvas approach for individual pages instead of a linear report layout, so it is worth considering the order in which the strategy story is presented. The aim is for the story to be engaging and to make sense; it needs to be constructed in a way that the reader can follow the structure and find his or her way around easily. In some cases this is best achieved by taking an organisation-wide perspective in telling the strategy journey story through its four stages; in others it might work better to adopt a themes or challenges approach for some of the stages.

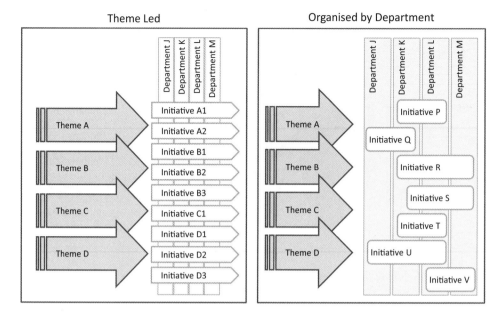

Figure 7.3 Organising strategic initiatives

Just as each organisation's strategy journey is different – as are the strategy journeys of an organisation at different times – so there is no 'best practice' format for the strategic plan documents that tell the stories of those journeys. My aim in this chapter has been to encourage readers to consider this as an opportunity to think creatively about how to develop such a document, to approach the challenge of articulating their organisation's strategy journey in a way that makes sense and brings it to life as a useful document that will guide people's decisions and motivate them to act.

Part III

WHAT MAKES AN EFFECTIVE STRATEGIC PLAN?

8

ENGAGEMENT

Part 1 of this book focused on deconstructing the somewhat daunting perceptions about strategic planning and replacing these with a 'first principles' approach that identified the four fundamental questions to be addressed in developing a strategic plan and the principal activities – strategising, organising, learning and leadership – through which an organisation can answer those questions. We looked at how the need to make sense of where the organisation is and where it wants to go is a powerful motivator driving people to work together on their organisation's 'strategy journey'.

In part 2 we considered several aspects of how to go about developing a strategic plan. We discussed the need to understand the context and how that influences how an organisation might go about its strategy journey. We considered the importance of questions and the value of conversations at the heart of that process and explored some practical aspects of facilitating these and using various tools and techniques to develop the rich content of a strategy journey. Finally, we looked at the creative challenge of telling the story of the strategy journey in a way that helped people make sense of where the organisation was heading and acted as a platform for action to help it achieve this.

This final part of the book will examine what makes a strategic plan effective. As we will see, this is not about the ability to predict the future, the accuracy of the projections or flawless implementation of the plan; in fact, a strategic plan can be effective without achieving any of these.

Understanding and ownership

Strategic planning is how the people in an organisation make sense of where it's going and how it's going to get there.

Sensemaking and the quest for meaning have featured throughout this book as important motivators for people, with an organisation's strategy journey being a collective endeavour to develop a common view about the organisation and its future. We have emphasised the importance of rich conversations and robust constructive challenge at a sufficiently deep level to ensure a shared understanding amongst those most directly involved in strategising, organising and leading during the strategy journey, and also that this understanding needs to be replicated across the organisation. Whilst others might not need to repeat the analysis and exploration that has led to the resulting strategies, to understand the thinking each individual needs to go through the same mental process to accept the assumptions, rationale and conclusions of each argument. Ideally this should happen during the development of the strategic plan, rather than relying on a strategic plan document, which then acts as a reminder of that thinking.

In practice, however, it is seldom possible to involve everyone in an organisation to that depth during the formulation of strategy and development of the plan. Content produced during this process can be an important way in which thinking can be shared as it is developing; even if it is modified subsequently, there is wider awareness of the questions that are being answered and an appreciation of the context and some of the aspects being considered.

In chapter 7 we discussed how a strategic plan document should articulate this thinking and make it easy to understand the rationale for what has been developed. This document plays a vital role as a platform for wider communication and reiteration of these arguments. However, a strategic plan document represents only a stepping stone in the organisation's overall strategy journey; there is still the implementation of the strategic plan to make happen. The strategic plan document is an important platform for this – but as the journey continues, so does the importance of the communicating and sharing of the strategy journey story as it evolves, and revisiting and reinforcing the reasoning. The need for rich conversations and answering questions continues.

Conversations are powerful. When the focus of an organisation is on the production of a strategic plan document, however well crafted, it can never be a substitute for continually talking, listening and learning about the organisation's strategy journey. Conversations help check understanding, and clarify, reiterate and revise when appropriate; they help embed the journey within the day-to-day life of the organisation.

Understanding the thinking is just the first stage in an individual's engagement with the organisation's strategy journey. There are several further stages we each progress through; we might understand the argument that has been made, but not agree with it (either its assumptions or its logic). If we do agree with the conclusion, do we support it? And if so, with what degree of ownership? Each of these stages involves both rational thinking and emotional engagement, as well as progressive commitment as one steps to the next level; there is a significant gulf between understanding an argument and taking ownership of it.

Both understanding and agreement are necessary for people to engage with a strategic plan. It is that emotional commitment to a rationally accepted argument that is essential for the strategic plan to be supported.

For a strategic plan to be effective, we need not just the commitment of an individual but organisation-wide ownership and commitment to the organisation's strategy journey. Every person in the organisation will make their own decisions as to which of the steps they reach along the stages from non-understanding to ownership. Whilst it might be desirable for everyone in the organisation to own and be fully committed to a strategic plan, in practice such an ambition is unlikely to be realised (there will always be someone who, for whatever reason, does not engage sufficiently with this). A realistic aim, though, is to achieve a critical mass of engaged and committed people in the organisation; as momentum builds, so the influence of those committed grows

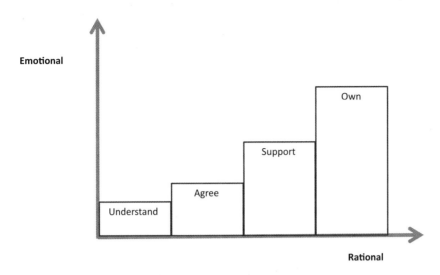

Figure 8.1 Steps to commitment

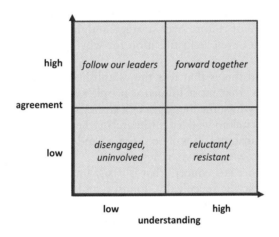

Figure 8.2 Agreement and understanding

amongst their peers and colleagues, prompting others to consider their own response, with social dynamics playing a part in both the rational and emotional dimensions. In complexity theory,[1] organisations are made up of complex responsive interactions between people; people relate to others via conversations, observed behaviours and the dynamics of power and social relationships. Arguably, an organisation's strategy journey is about shaping the framework for those interactions, working out the patterns and paths the organisation wishes to follow. Such a view reinforces the idea that strategic planning is not a mechanistic, analytical process that can be project managed, but a journey that people in the organisation are motivated to decide to take together.

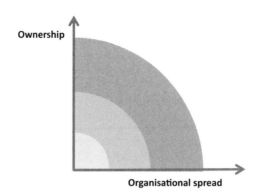

Figure 8.3 Organisational ownership

Strategy and culture

'Culture eats strategy for breakfast' (or 'for lunch', depending on which version of the often-repeated phrase one prefers). Usually attributed as a verbal quote by Peter Drucker (the evidence is from secondary sources), this phrase is used by some to assert the dominant influence of culture over strategy and, hence, to explain why strategies can fail (and sometimes even as justification for why they think strategic planning is a waste of time!).

The thinking behind this is that it is the established patterns of relationships and 'ways of doing things' that most influence people's attitudes and behaviours in an organisation and that whilst the messages of a strategic plan might be understood and its rationale and intent acknowledged, ultimately (when the individual or organisation is under pressure, for instance) it will be the tried and tested patterns that people will revert to in deciding how to behave or act.

Organisational culture is a concept that is easily understood but difficult to define, and even harder to describe specifically. Johnson and Scholes[2] introduce a very helpful model, the cultural web, to help organisations articulate the influences on their culture. In this model, it is not just the organisation structures, the formal policies and processes and the power relationships, but also the established routines and rituals, the symbols and the stories that are used as examples – together these shape how people understand the nature of the organisation and hence how they behave. The 'taken for granted' assumptions underlying these can be distilled into a summary 'paradigm' that characterises the essence of an organisation's culture – but it is the combined spheres of influence and layers of attitudes and behaviours that together determine and act to reinforce the culture.

Changing the culture in an organisation requires a sustained effort to change these established patterns by signalling and reinforcing different values and establishing new patterns across all these spheres. Such changes can be subtle – leaders and influencers in the organisation adopting different behaviours, reinforced by continual conversations – or symbolic, such as the removal from positions of influence of those not demonstrating the agreed-upon values or a new remuneration strategy that rewards in ways that support the desired behaviours. But they need to be applied in all the culture-influencing spheres in the cultural web, and they need to be applied consistently and continually until the old patterns are replaced and the new ones established. A useful analogy is that of changing the course of a stream: not only do we need to take some action to divert the water initially, but we need to make sure the water continues to flow into the new channel and not revert to its established previous water course by blocking the flow to the latter and ensuring there is sufficient pressure to force the flow into the new channel and that this does not silt up.

Culture is, then, a powerful influence on what happens in an organisation. It is easy to see how such an invisible magnetic field can attract people back to well-worn patterns even when a rational and accepted strategy sets a different path. No wonder the phrase 'culture eats strategy' has such credence.

However, an effective strategic plan takes account of the organisation's culture. Indeed, it is developed in the knowledge of the organisation's culture. Returning to our journey analogy, those planning and setting out together on a journey do so aware of what they know about the relationships and dynamics within the group and how this might affect their journey. Along the way they will discover more, as difficulties are encountered and decisions made, and as they learn more from the many conversations. It is an element of leadership of the journey that this learning will shape how to approach future stages, and at times there might be decisions made to change the way in which the journey continues.

A strategy journey considers the organisation's culture, its values and its purpose. At the deepest, most elemental level an organisation's strategy is about how it sees itself (or more accurately, how the people in the organisation perceive it and how they relate to it) and how it defines its future. Inherent in this is the purpose of the organisation, what it sees as its role and mission to achieve, why it exists, the values that will guide its actions and the principles by which it will operate. We have seen how powerful is the need for people to make sense of their situation: their relationship with their organisation, how they see their role within the organisation and their social interaction with others in the organisation all contribute to this and to how they see themselves and define their identity. Culture is the 'magnetic field' that shapes the patterns of relationships and paths within the organisation; strategy is the evolving story the organisation tells itself to explain what it is and where it is heading and how people in the organisation make sense of this.

So strategy is about culture. It is about understanding and articulating the organisation's purpose, its values, and determining the principles by which it will operate consistent with these. During the course of a strategy journey an organisation might realise that there were issues with its current culture that it needed to address or that the organisation's values needed restating and reinforcing; such initiatives become a part of the strategic plan. Or it might be that such concerns were part of the context prompting the organisation to undertake a strategy journey in order to work out what its values should be and how to establish them. Newly formed organisations, or those facing new circumstances or whose identity is changing, might want to engage people in a collective process to define the organisation's purpose, to help make sense of the next phase of the organisation's development. Culture does not eat an effective strategy for supper or any other meal; instead they set off together on the organisation's strategy journey as people work out what new paths they might need to take.

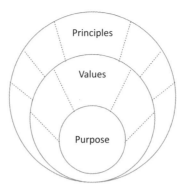

Figure 8.4 Purpose, values and principles

A platform for action

If conversations are powerful, actions are more so. The implication of an action inconsistent with a stated intent is to undermine credibility and trust. Organisational culture
is determined by what happens rather than how it is described; values are reinforced
by behaviours as well as words, and principles are statements on which to base decisions and to be acted upon.

An effective strategic plan is a platform for action. On one level it sets out how
the organisation plans to achieve its strategic objectives through specific initiatives,
and implementing these will be a priority across the organisation. Understanding the
rationale by which these were developed will help the organisation update or modify
these plans when something changes. If the objective is clear, adapting how this might
be achieved will be much easier if setbacks are encountered. On another level, how
the strategic plan articulates the purpose, values and principles of the organisation can
provide a clear framework to which people in the organisation can refer when making
decisions; these provide the touchstones by which actions and behaviours should be
judged.

It is of course the strategy journey, and not just a strategic plan document, that
makes this possible. The depth of discussion and debate and the drive for clarity and
shared meaning contribute to a fundamental understanding of what the organisation
is and what it wants to be. In our discussion about engagement we considered the
progression from rational understanding to ownership and commitment, as well as
embedding this across the organisation: can this become a platform from which people make decisions and act? If people in an organisation fully understand the values
and principles underpinning the organisation's strategic plan, can they act on these?
Have they the confidence, encouraged and enabled by the organisation, to take the
initiative based on this? Has their participation in their organisation's strategy journey
given them the ability, and the remit, to act?

This is a measure not only of an effective strategic plan, but also of an organisation
that trusts its people and through its strategy journey provides the platform for them
to contribute fully to helping it realise its vision and achieve its strategic objectives.

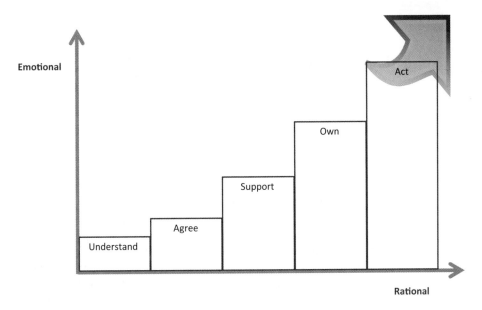

Figure 8.5 Platform for action

Notes

1 See for example Stacey R., *Strategic Management and Organisational Dynamics* (5th edition), Financial Times Prentice Hall, Harlow, UK, 2007
2 Johnson G., Scholes K. and Whittington R., *Exploring Corporate Strategy* (7th edition), Financial Times Prentice Hall, Harlow, UK, 2006

9

IMPLEMENTATION

One of the frequent comments made about strategic planning is that 'x per cent of strategic plans fail through poor implementation', where the magnitude of the x per cent quoted (usually between 66 per cent and 90 per cent) varies depending on the research report, survey of chief executives or business magazine article recently read. Irrespective of the statistical accuracy or research methods used, the message is very clear: for many organisations implementation is the Achilles' heel of their strategic plans. In this chapter we will consider some of the reasons for this and what organisations might do to help implement their strategic plan effectively.

Making it happen

Developing a strategic plan and implementing it are two very different challenges. Formulating strategy is exciting and stimulating – those involved are deciding the future of their organisation. It requires critical thinking and deep discussion, usually concentrated into an intensive few months. The perspective is of the 'bigger picture' and the medium to long term; planning how to implement the strategy is about directing the resources of the organisation. The core of the work tends to be undertaken by a relatively small group including the senior levels of the organisation, with key stakeholders taking a keen interest.

Implementing a strategic plan involves the entire organisation. The focus is on doing: organising resources to achieve an appropriate balance with day-to-day operational work, ensuring people are working well together, managing progress and overcoming obstacles. It requires a sustained effort at all levels of the organisation over a few years, with board-level interest being more about the results than the detail.

Imagine being one of the executive team leading the organisation through the strategic planning process. Over the past few months you have put a lot of your time and energy – individually as well as collectively – into debating, working through issues, shaping the strategic direction, considering how to achieve it, gaining agreement and commitment. You have worked to help develop a document that crystallises this work, articulating the strategy and setting out how the organisation should go about implementing it; you have tried to address all the challenges and consider the risks, and now at last there has been formal approval and sign-off, and the document has been sent to all interested stakeholders. It is an achievement, a milestone has been reached – and you are mentally and physically drained. It will be a welcome change to come into work tomorrow and not have to worry about the strategic plan, turning your attention to some of the less challenging but important operational issues that you have put to one side over the intense past few weeks.

Having briefly caught your strategic planning breath, so to speak, you approach the next few weeks with renewed energy, even if it is not quite as intense and all-consuming as when you were in the final stages of developing the strategic plan (which by now has been acclaimed as good work by some key senior people). These next few weeks are about communicating the strategic plan throughout the organisation, making sure people understand the rationale as well as the direction and the objectives. The workshops, the meetings, the discussions are positive but hard work; there are questions and challenges and some objections to overcome. You are also busy setting up the strategic initiative projects, forming the steering groups, working out progress measures and how they are reported. There is much to work out – somehow the detail is more complicated than the simple way in which it was expressed in the strategic plan document; there are negotiations with departments, concerns about the impact on operational work and external help to be arranged in some areas. Project governance structures are put in place, the workgroups are well briefed. The energy and effort invested by you and your executive team colleagues in developing the strategic plan and organising resources have now been transferred to others working across the organisation. It is now up to them to get on with it, with progress being monitored through the processes that have been put in place.

Roll forward a year, and we find that progress has been mixed. After a promising start some groups are now behind on the original timetable, and some projects are not delivering the results expected. Some pressing operational issues have required resources to be reallocated to deal with these, and the commitment behind one strategic initiative is waning as doubts develop about whether it is the right approach, especially given increased uncertainty about the potential impact of a regulatory review. The executive team decide to restructure and relaunch some of the projects, whilst the second annual budget-setting process has required some tough decisions about priorities. The strategic plan has assumed a secondary profile, being mentioned occasionally only in general terms.

Six months later when the newly appointed non-executive directors review the organisation's progress against the strategic plan document there appears to be a significant gap between the current reality and the plan, and they struggle to reconcile what is actually happening in the organisation with the strategic framework outlined less than two years previously.

Such a gulf between the organisation's strategic plan and its current situation would seem to imply that this is one of the x per cent of plans that has failed through poor implementation. We will return to this later in the chapter, but for now I want to focus on one particular aspect of this example.

Organisational energy

At the beginning of this section we discussed the differences between developing a strategic plan and implementing it, including differences in the intensity and type of the work and the involvement of people in the organisation. In the earlier example we saw how the energy of the executive team member flowed and ebbed across the various phases and similarly how the nature of the executive team's involvement changed too. Although they had put in considerable effort to ensure the strategic plan was understood widely across the organisation, and they had worked hard to set up the strategic initiative projects, that energy was not sustained subsequently; despite well-thought-through project governance and reporting structures, in hindsight neither the required energy nor focus was maintained, nor the continual reinforcement of the relationship of the work to the strategic plan (and not just to the specific strategic initiatives, but also to the strategic thinking from which they developed). Leadership in a strategy journey applies not just to the formulation of strategy and organising how this can be achieved, but also to making it happen.

Effective implementation of a strategic plan requires the investment of such sustained effort. Figure 9.1 illustrates conceptually how the energy across the organisation changes in the example and how this compares to an ideal trajectory where the executive team (in this case) continues to give implementation of the strategic plan the same actual priority as they invested in developing the plan.

As an analogy, in the prior example consider the communication of the strategic plan across the organisation and the establishment of the strategic initiative projects as being like throwing a stone in a pool; there is energy in the splash and the waves as they spread across the pool, but without further injections of energy these will soon become mere ripples and eventually disappear (even though the executive team believes it has generated the required energy with the first stone).

Consider also our discussion in chapter 7 about organisational culture and how important actions and behaviours are in defining and reinforcing this. Continual reference to the strategic plan throughout the organisation, the continuing visible prioritisation of its implementation by the organisation's leaders and influencers investing their own time and energy – these are important organisational culture 'signals' that influence the attitudes and behaviours that people in the organisation will themselves choose. This illustrates again the synergetic relationship between organisational culture and strategy.

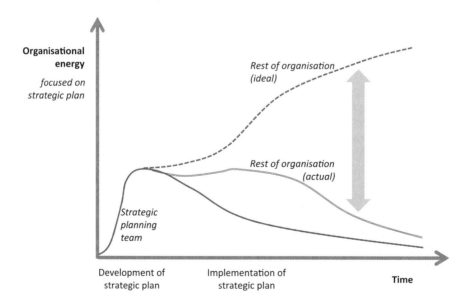

Figure 9.1 Sustaining organisational energy

Following through

Another challenge illustrated in our example concerned investing sufficient resources to implement strategic initiatives whilst also meeting 'day-to-day' operational requirements, and how these were rebalanced to meet more immediate priorities, with the consequent slippage on achieving progress on those initiatives.

There are never enough resources to do everything an organisation might want to do. Deciding how to allocate resources – people, time, energy, facilities – is a continual challenge. Planning and then organising these is a vital part of the strategy journey, working out just what is needed for the organisation to get to where it wants to go next.

The first stage in this is to consider just what the principal activities are which the organisation needs to undertake to achieve its strategic objectives. We have discussed the idea of strategic themes and initiatives as constructs to help provide a framework and helpful focus for the strategic plan. We have also considered the tensions that exist between the need to expend resources on new strategic projects and the more operational 'day job'. But to consider the organisation's resources and how these are allocated and prioritised, it is necessary to take an holistic view; what are the overall requirements of the organisation, what is achievable realistically (including financially), how might these change over the course of implementing the strategic plan? These questions are all part of answering 'How do we get there?' during the development of the strategic plan; they will lead to deciding what additional resources might be required, what skills and capabilities are needed and how these vary over time. The model that is developed to help work this out – however approximate or detailed – will be based on assumptions and projections; it provides a working tool for the organisation to help identify its overall resource requirements. Although this is likely to be refined and developed over time, it is a framework for re-considering these when appropriate as changes occur.

This overview approach to the organisation's overall activities and resource needs is consistent with viewing this as a strategy journey that involves the whole organisation, and not just the advance party blazing the trail for everyone else to follow. Similarly the way in which these principal activities are framed is important in how they are positioned within the scope of the organisation's total activity and how new initiatives are perceived to fit with current operational work. For example, are the strategic initiatives seen as being distinct from 'business as usual', with work on these organised separately from operational activities (perhaps in the case of ventures into new markets or developments requiring new information and infrastructure systems)? Or are the strategic initiatives essentially ways in which the organisation will develop across all parts of the business (for example, a new values-based rewards and remuneration strategy)? Maybe there are several themes of strategic development, each of which includes elements of the current operational activity plus developmental initiatives (such as if the themes were closely aligned to defined functions within the organisation)?

However the organisation chooses to frame its principal activities, it is important that all are included. This avoids a dichotomy between 'strategic' work and 'operational' work when considering the organisation's resource requirements and how these should be allocated and prioritised. Maintaining this total view, using the framework

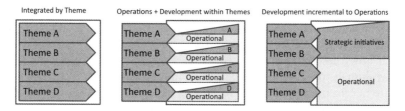

Figure 9.2 Strategic initiatives and operational activities

and working model that have been developed to consider whether these resource allocations need to change in the light of developments and reviewing these in the context of the organisation's strategic plan, will help avoid the perception of apparent disjoints and drift from the plan that we saw in the example earlier in this chapter. It is also important that any revisions are linked to the strategic plan through a narrative that explains the thinking behind these.

Strategic initiatives can often be associated with major organisational changes, either explicitly or as an aspect of how a strategic objective will be achieved. The complexity of organisational change, and the energy needed to effect this, are easily underestimated (sometimes with disastrous results; there are many examples of organisations that have embarked on overambitious projects, where mergers have failed to deliver the expected benefits and where the impact on people has been very damaging).

Let us consider this further. Individuals and groups can respond to changes in various ways, depending on the impact on them personally and on their work. There are several very helpful models about change,[1] including the stages that people can go through in coming to terms with major change and how organisations can manage the process. But for the purposes of this discussion we will assume that this is a significant but otherwise straightforward change and will use our simple rational acceptance/emotional embedding 'steps to commitment' model to indicate the journey every individual needs to make from understanding to ownership before acting on the change with their full energy. They then need to learn how to implement the change – the knowledge about how to act – and the final stage is about doing, trying, developing competence and then becoming proficient in the new ways of doing things.

Just as when we discussed engagement in the context of an effective strategic plan, this individual understanding-to-ownership process, and then the learning followed by the trying and the development of competency, has to be replicated across the organisation until the 'critical momentum' to establish the change is achieved.

Although this is an indicative conceptual model, it illustrates the significant investment of organisational energy required to implement changes. In cases that are more complex, or where acceptance of change by individuals or groups is more difficult, the energy and other resources required are much greater. It is easy to underestimate the energy and time needed to reach 'critical momentum' for changes to be established in an organisation.

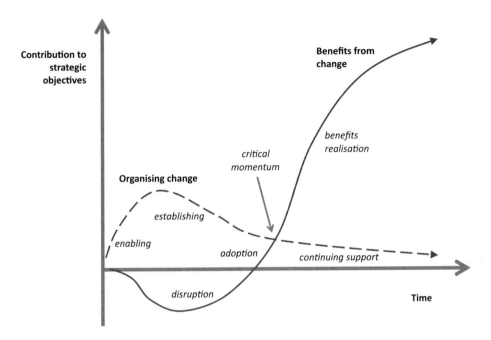

Figure 9.3 Change energy model

A brief digression about terminology: 'change management' is the phrase often used to discuss what an organisation needs to do to establish significant change. However, the impression given by this is of a structured programme of activities applied to people in the organisation to achieve a pre-determined change objective. Change can happen in other ways, though, as people adapt to events, from self-determined initiatives or to seize new opportunities; the stimulus can arise in any part of the organisation. Change is not always top-down, and neither is it always as a result of choice. I prefer to use the term 'managing change' as this is applicable to any of these circumstances, determined or reactive, top-down or self-initiated. It is an organisational capability to which anyone can contribute. Indeed, it can be seen as a collective activity towards a common goal to successfully assimilate change within the organisation.

We discussed earlier in this chapter the need to continually refresh the energy driving implementation of a strategic plan, and in chapter 8 we considered how consistent actions, behaviours and conversations help establish or reinforce the culture of an organisation. The same reasoning can be applied to a strategic plan: continually talking about it, demonstrating how decisions and actions are consistent with the strategy and principles in the plan, referring to the strategic themes and presenting arguments and reporting information using the framework developed in the plan – these will help keep it at the forefront of people's thinking. Telling people how the organisation is performing is healthy, and letting them know how it is developing, about its progress towards its strategic goals, reinforces focus on the strategic plan.

This continual reference to the strategic plan helps make it as much a part of the organisation's core work as its day-to-day operational activities. Indeed, undertaking those activities is a part of implementing the strategic plan, helping the organisation achieve its objectives. Conversations and actions demonstrate that it is important and reinforce commitment; interest, encouragement and thanks impart energy. A strategic plan that is at the heart of an organisation, that becomes a strategy journey being undertaken by everyone in the organisation, is going to be much more effective than a document that sits on a shelf, however many boxes it ticked when it was produced.

Strategic management

How do you measure progress when implementing a strategic plan? Here are two examples to illustrate alternative ways of approaching this:

The development process of Organisation M's strategic plan is complete; a document summarising it has been produced (with versions adapted to various stakeholder audiences), and in-depth discussions about it have occurred throughout the organisation. The focus is now on carrying forward the momentum of the past few months into setting up the implementation phase, with a strong commitment to making the plan happen and a determination that this organisation's strategic plan will not founder during implementation.

A robust governance structure has been established, with a programme team coordinating the various strategic initiative workstreams, steering groups with board-level representation and cross-functional project teams already formed and starting to meet. The executive team has brought in programme management expertise to assist with project coordination and reporting. The project groups consider their briefs and work out how they will approach this and go about their tasks. There is some discussion about clarification, and in some cases the scope was changed to include aspects that had not been considered initially. Project plans and Gantt charts have been developed and published, and the work begins.

One of the first requests from the board was for a way for them to be able to review progress; they were looking for visibility and simplicity of progress reports across all projects, the highlighting of major issues and key measures for each initiative that would track improvements in organisational performance towards the strategic objectives set out in the strategic plan document. The project groups responded by developing a comprehensive suite of measures and reports that would give a thorough assessment of what they had achieved; the coordinating programme team then worked on these and produced an impressive monthly report document drawing out the key points in a summary but enabling the board to scrutinise the supporting information for each project, with colourful charts helping illustrate this. The board gave this their detailed attention, reflecting their commitment to the strategic plan and their duties in overseeing the organisation's strategy (they particularly liked the 'red-amber-green traffic lights' scales that were used to show variances against targets), and considerable effort was expended each month by the project groups and the programme team in collating and assessing the information.

Organisation N's approach to implementing their strategic plan was to establish steering groups to champion and progress each of the five strategic themes that they had developed. These included a combination of strategic development initiatives and aspects of current operational activities. For some of the development initiatives, workgroups were established to lead this work across the organisation, whilst for others it was felt more appropriate to use a project management approach. The executive team worked very closely with the five steering groups – a member of the team worked in each group – and at an early stage they agreed upon two actions they felt were essential: to ensure regular, coordinated updates to everyone in the organisation about progress in implementing the strategic plan; and to decide on some simple measures fundamental to the strategy that would show the organisation's progress towards its objectives. The former was straightforward: people throughout the organisation knew about the themes, they understood the thinking behind them, and the executive team reinforced this by using the same framework of themes and high-level objectives and the same phrases that had been used in the development of the strategic plan (reiterated often as it was being developed). The messages were simple but honest (there was to be no 'glossing over' of problems or setbacks), a consistent format was used that provided continuity and all formal and informal channels and media were used. People were encouraged to contribute, to ask questions – anybody could post comments or updates on the organisation's internal social media platforms; there was a 'buzz' about the work, lots of interaction and involvement – it felt almost like fun . . .

Deciding on the strategic measures was a tougher challenge. They needed to be what really mattered for each strategic theme, measures that were fundamental to the strategic objective. There would be several factors contributing to this, and factors contributing to each of these in turn; in this 'hierarchy of factors' each one has associated measures – and in the work of the strategic theme groups these needed to have high visibility – but it was the key strategic measures that the executive team wanted to focus on first, with the confidence that they could talk to the steering groups and find out more detail if they needed to. The culture of Organisation N was one of trust and support, and the executive team felt no need to repeat the detailed analysis of the strategic theme steering groups. Instead, they could choose to use their time and energy to lend support on any particularly challenging or complex issue.

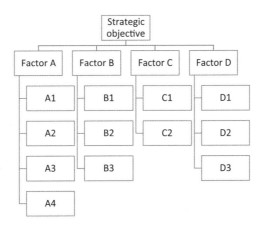

Figure 9.4 Strategic measures

Having thought through what strategic measures were appropriate for each theme to monitor progress towards achieving the strategic objectives, and having had in-depth discussions with the steering groups, the executive team developed a one-page report to act as a starting point for a two-hour workshop with the board each quarter. This included a 'Strategic Scorecard'[2] that showed the track of progress in each theme towards the strategic objective using the measures devised, together with brief bullet-point commentary to help explain each one. Each workshop would discuss the summary, then focus on two specific issues that had been highlighted as causing concern or needing support or guidance, with other members from the relevant steering group taking part in these discussions as appropriate. (This did not exclude the opportunity to convene other meetings to deal with any urgent and critical issues, as would happen if any such situation arose; however, the longer-term nature of these strategic themes meant that such circumstances would be exceptional.) The emphasis was on working together to understand and resolve issues, and the steering groups and executive team worked hard developing each quarterly report to ensure there was good preparation for a focused and well-informed discussion at the workshop.

Neither of our two organisations' approaches is necessarily 'wrong'; each has its strengths as well as its risks, and the approach chosen might suit that organisation's 'way of doing things'. Culture plays a significant role in influencing how an organisation manages the implementation phase of its strategic plan in particular – the sustained involvement of people across the organisation over many months means that cultural norms are very likely to shape actions and behaviours and hence the approach that is taken to implementing the strategic plan. However, their respective approaches might result in differing degrees of effectiveness in implementing their strategic plans.

The focus in Organisation M is on the projects and the details of their progress: how these link to the strategic objectives could quite easily be subsumed under the amount of data. The frequent collation of this data will take up a lot of resources. Furthermore, the analysis is in effect being undertaken at board level rather than the board focusing its attention on the results of that analysis and what they can do to help the organisation overcome obstacles and challenges; if the board sees its primary role as holding the executive team to account, then it is that team that needs to take responsibility instead for unblocking issues. In such an organisational culture there could be a lot of time and effort expended on people and teams defending their positions, 'justifying' any perceived underachievement or slippage in progress. Making excuses and prioritising self-protection over understanding and tacking the issues increases the likelihood of such an organisation's strategic plan not being implemented effectively.

Figure 9.5 Strategic Scorecard

Organisation N, on the other hand, has thought through its approach to defining its strategic measures and how it intends to use these. There is a simple, clear alignment to its strategic objectives and the way in which it has framed these through strategic themes. There is a consistency and hence reinforcement in the way in which it has organised to implement the plan and how it has decided to communicate its progress across the organisation. Engagement with people is strong; conversations about the strategic plan are continual and are matched by actions, with encouragement to contribute increasing the 'critical momentum'. The culture of openness and support leads to a collective focus on tackling issues and overcoming setbacks, and the expertise and resources of the organisation are being used appropriately, with effective conversations ensuring the flow and sharing of information. There are some risks in this approach – someone might try to take advantage of the trust and either inadvertently or deliberately mislead. But the strength of the culture including the open involvement of others reduces the likelihood of this either happening or of it not being noticed. Of course, there can always be events that are unpredicted or outside of Organisation N's control or influence that could affect the implementation of its strategic plan, but the approach it has adopted increases its likelihood of succeeding.

Critical measures

Measuring what really matters is important; there might be many contributing factors, but focusing on what is most important will lead to actions that support the achievement of this. Returning to the example from my own experience with GrandMet Brewing that I quoted in chapter 6, prior to reviewing the strategy the company's marketing focus had been on measuring the number of stockists of each beer brand. Promotions were aimed at encouraging pub landlords and bar managers to agree to stock the brand, and the sales force was set targets and incentivised on the number of new beer taps installed as a result. The technical services team then had to arrange to visit and install the dispensing equipment, including the branded beer cowls or hand pumps; they were put under pressure by the sales force to complete this before the deadline for the incentive, resulting in high payments for overtime and scheduling inefficiencies.

All the relevant functions and departments of the organisation were aligned behind this activity, and the results were given a high internal profile. The number of beer taps of a particular brand installed during a particular period was the strategic measure the organisation had chosen to monitor its progress towards achieving its sales and market share objectives for its major brands.

But there was a problem with this. Despite fluctuations from month to month, there was much less overall increase in brand distribution and sales over the course of a year. After talking – and listening – to customers and the sales force, what was really happening became clear: bar owners were taking advantage of the promotional incentives and price deals on offer to install whatever brand was being featured that month as a replacement for another that was already on the bar. If that happened to be a GrandMet Brewing brand, the net result was that total sales remained unchanged – unless the brand installed happened to be more popular with the bar's customers, in which case it was likely to remain part of the bar's portfolio of draught beers.

Otherwise, the recently installed brand would be replaced by whatever was being promoted next – with the technicians having to make another visit to remove the dispensing equipment, taps, fonts and cowls. The net effect of this churn was that considerable activity, resources and money were being expended by the organisation to little sustained longer-term benefit in achieving its strategic objectives. Whilst what was being measured was a factor contributing to the objective, it was not the right strategic measure and had resulted in costly inefficiencies as well as ineffective implementation of the company's marketing strategy. The ensuing review of strategy considered customer perspectives and needs and how to achieve the strategic objectives through developing a different type of longer-term relationship with them, including focusing on more appropriate strategic measures.

By having a clear link to the strategic objectives, the measures that Organisation N has developed have an important advantage in that they will be consistent through the lifetime of the strategic plan, even if time scales slip or there are changes to some of the initiatives. It is the structured relationships as illustrated in the 'hierarchy of factors' diagram (Figure 9.4) earlier in this chapter that mean that the implications of any change can be worked through to see what effect this might have on other measures: there is a consistency to the set of measures which enables changes to be explained and understood.

This applies also to the connectedness between the various elements of a strategic plan. There should be a flow of thinking from the assessment of where the organisation is now to where it wants to get to, how it is going to get there and what it is going to do to make that happen. Then when something changes – as is bound to happen – the thinking can be retraced to work through the implications and decide what might need to be revised or re-thought. Adapting to changes is a vital aspect of strategic management. In some respects a strategic plan can be likened to a system, to patterns of thinking; understanding how changes in one part affect the other elements, considering how to adapt the whole whilst maintaining the integrity of the connections, is part of the leadership skills we highlighted as one of the key organisational capabilities required on a strategy journey.

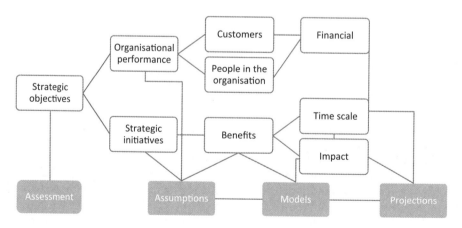

Figure 9.6 Strategic plan as system

Let us return briefly to the example we introduced at the beginning of this chapter, where the new non-executive directors found what appeared to be a significant gap between what was happening in the organisation and the strategic plan that had been developed less than two years previously. Is this an example of the failed implementation of a strategic plan?

There are some concerning signs: some of the projects are behind schedule or failing to achieve the targeted benefits; one strategic initiative appears to be foundering on doubts about whether its original rationale is still applicable; and the budget revisions have resulted in a big gap between the latest financial projections and those mapped out originally during the development of the strategic plan. Indeed, the strategic plan might well have to be consigned to the paper shredder and judged a failure.

However, this is not necessarily the case. What has certainly happened here is that the connection of decisions and changes to the strategic plan has been lost. Various parts of the story have been changed without it being obvious whether they still fit with the narrative that was developed earlier. It is possible that the decisions that have been taken are entirely consistent with the thinking in the strategic plan – that what has happened is that changes have been made without visibly 'joining up the thinking' and explaining them with reference to the plan; the organisation has had to change its route on its strategy journey because of difficulties it has encountered on a particular stage, but its direction and intended destination remain the same, although it might take it longer to reach it and via a different route for part of the journey. If this is the case, then the failure is one of strategic management to explain the reasons for the changes in the context of the strategic plan, to reassert the continuing commitment to the organisation's strategic objectives and demonstrate that the revised implementation plan is consistent with the thinking and the principles developed when the organisation was starting out on its strategy journey.

Notes

1   See for example: Kotter J., *Leading Change*, Harvard Business School Press, Boston, 1996; Bridges W., *Managing Transitions: Making the Most of Change* (3rd edition), Nicholas Brealey Publishing, London, 2009; Kubler-Ross E., *On Death & Dying* (40th anniversary edition), Routledge, Abingdon, UK, 2008
2   The Balanced Scorecard concept was pioneered by Kaplan and Norton – see Kaplan R. and Norton D., *The Balanced Scorecard: Translating Strategy into Action*, Harvard Business Review Press, Boston, 1996

10

REVIEW

In the previous two chapters we have discussed the importance of achieving understanding and ownership of the strategic plan across the organisation and developing an organisation-wide critical momentum behind its implementation. We saw that the way in which work on strategic initiatives is organised, and how progress is measured, needs to be thought through to ensure a clear focus on the strategic objectives, enabling the organisation to adapt these if circumstances require. Using the objectives and themes of the strategic plan as a consistent frame of reference in conversations and actions will continually reinforce its position at the heart of the organisation and will reinforce the energy and focus needed to sustain implementation.

Monitoring progress continually is essential; critically reviewing the plan periodically is vital.

An organisation's strategic plan is about its future. It is at the heart of the organisation – yet often it seems to be treated almost as supplementary to the organisation's ongoing operational activities, rather than encompassing these. It is easy to see how those initiatives designed to develop the organisation's ability to achieve its strategic goals can be viewed as incremental, but reaching the desired destination requires the contribution and involvement of the organisation as a whole. That is why it needs to be the central topic in the organisation's 'conversation', rather than an occasional agenda item at board meetings.

From this perspective it makes sense to use the framework of the strategic plan to review organisational performance and progress on a regular basis, both informally and formally. But even without such an holistic philosophy it is crucial that the organisation examine its strategic plan at least once a year. Long gone are the years (assuming they ever existed) when a five-year plan would map the expansion of a business in an established industry operating in growing but stable markets. With continual, rapid (and to some extent unpredictable) change being the widely held model for our times, to forget, omit or fail to check that the assumptions made a year or so previously (and upon which the organisation has planned its future) are still correct seems difficult to excuse. It makes sense too to revisit the thinking by which the strategic plan developed – perhaps not in a fundamental way, starting again and replicating the intensive formulation of strategy, but as a minimum to check that the rationale is still valid. Senior-level responsibility and engagement in this, and summarising the review in a formal way, will help ensure that this is given priority, and sharing this with others in the organisation and with key stakeholders will help reinforce the importance and commitment given by the organisation to its continuing strategy journey.

Sensing the signs

So what could possibly go wrong? Throughout this book we have considered several of the pitfalls, illustrated in the examples provided. It might be instructive at this point to list a few of the reasons strategic plans fail to be effective:

1 Some of the key assumptions turn out to be inaccurate (quantitative) or did not happen (qualitative). This can apply to the projections or to the strategy (which can have a more significant impact).
2 The model of 'how we see things' turns out to be incorrect. Again, this can apply critically to the assessment of the organisation's position relative to its markets and competitors which formed the basis for developing the strategy.
3 The strategy chosen was not effective. Often this is due to either of the two previous reasons, but it can sometimes be the result of a flaw in the strategic thinking.
4 We didn't implement the strategy as planned/well enough/quickly enough.
5 We didn't follow-through our strategy consistently. So this is not a failure of the strategy, just that – for whatever reason – the organisation did not execute it well.
6 We underestimated x or overestimated y (often in terms of a competitor's capabilities or response, x, or our own organisation's, y, but this can also apply in the case of the impact of legislation or regulation).
7 We weren't committed to it. This can apply to the organisation as a whole or an influential section of the organisation. It could have been due to a lack of conviction or support initially, or doubts might have developed over time.
8 The strategic plan has 'run out of steam' or has become less relevant – or people have lost connection with it.
9 Events happened which were not foreseen, either externally or within the organisation.
10 We didn't adapt/change our strategy when A happened or we saw that B wasn't working.

A combination of these reasons might apply (several are interrelated). Regular, formal critical but constructive reviews of progress in implementing the strategic plan will help detect some of these factors, such as the assumptions or projection models. However, I want to focus in particular on the latter three and what happens when things change or don't go according to plan.

It is easy to think that you're right. So much thinking, discussion and debate have gone into formulating the strategy and developing the organisation's strategic plan. The analysis is robust; the strategic options were evaluated thoroughly and projection models were developed, scenarios tested and risks assessed – with healthy challenge at every stage. You and your colleagues worked hard at sharing the thinking and organising how to implement the plan. The process was intense, but stimulating, and it feels great to have the organisation now focused on some clear strategic objectives and energised to achieve them. The strategising is complete; it's now all down to the implementation.

Except that's not all there is to it. An aspect of strategic leadership is to continually monitor and assess – not just the progress of the various strategic initiatives and projects, and not just the measures associated with achievement of the organisation's strategic objectives, but to look beyond these into what might be happening in the external environment and beneath these to sense what is happening within the organisation.

The organisation is continuing its strategy journey. It now has an intended destination, and has mapped out the route and planned how it will undertake the journey, but it still has to travel along those paths and get there safely. Although there is a clear plan, and the motivation to succeed, the organisation will still need to be alert to what might occur. There will be obstacles and difficult terrain to be negotiated; both the middle distance and the horizon need to be scanned to spot potential difficulties or opportunities, and the health and spirit of those travelling need to be monitored. Being aware of the situation, alert to signs of change and sensitive to shifts in the mood of the organisation are key attributes of leadership; applied to the organisation's strategy journey they will help identify early any potential issues that might affect progress.

Whilst all the reasons listed earlier why strategic plans might fail to be effective can be identified with hindsight, alertness and sensitivity within the organisation to any changes in its external or internal circumstances might help it respond more quickly. In the natural world, organisms have developed acutely sensitive 'antennae' mechanisms to be alert to predators or prey or changes in conditions that require them to shelter. Organisations need to maintain such continual alertness and sensitivity to changes that might potentially affect them on their strategy journeys.

This sensitivity applies just as much internally as externally. One of the attributes of leadership is to be continually assessing the 'health' of the organisation, as well as its performance. Performance can be measured in the results achieved; organisational health is more about how well the organisation is working, its functions, processes and relationships, and how people are working within it and engaging with it. Much of this is about observing when some of these are not functioning smoothly and efficiently and also sensing the mood, being tuned in to pick up any issues from conversations, behaviours and attitudes.

This can happen with the organisation's strategy journey. As we have seen in the example in chapter 9, people can lose connection with the strategic plan; it might be implicitly assumed rather than explicitly discussed, or it could have slipped from the conversational agenda and focus of the organisation, no longer a priority concern. The impetus has gone, or the strategic plan is running out of steam or losing its relevance. It is time to revitalise, refresh, refocus or renew the organisation's strategy journey.

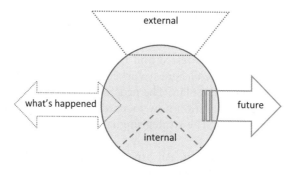

Figure 10.1 Organisational alertness

The agile organisation

A frequently heard criticism of strategic planning is that the continually changing circumstances and challenges faced by organisations nowadays require fast
responses, that longer-term projections and planning are of little use given the
pace of change.

Consider two types of journey. In the first, knowledge about the terrain is good.
The travel party will be crossing a plain with few undulations, and visibility is
expected to be clear so anything approaching will be spotted in good time. There
are a few known obstacles along the planned route such as rivers to be crossed, and
in its planning the expedition equips itself with planks and rope so it can construct
bridges. Preparations for the journey are thorough, with milestones targeted, provisions obtained and supply logistics arranged. Of course, people expect that there
will be some problems along the way – stretches that are harder to traverse, people
falling ill – and the route might need to be modified and the journey take a bit longer
as a result; there could always be earthquakes or floods, but such natural disasters
have been rare.

The second journey requires different preparations. The direction to the destination is known, but the route is less well defined. The territory is uncharted, although
the team has thought of the types of obstacles that are likely to be encountered. Its
preparations include working out how to deal as a group with what they encounter,
the channels of communication, the decision-making process. They also train to
develop skills they might need – the principles and practice of bridge construction,
applying these to rope bridges as well as wooden ones – and in how to be resourceful
in finding materials in the types of terrain they will be crossing. The team works on
its fitness and ability to respond and how they will equip themselves – orienteering
skills and robust rough-terrain running shoes rather than hiking boots and heavy
rucksacks.

The first journey is like the 'traditional' view of strategic planning, with thorough, detailed planning to execute a clearly mapped route. The second journey
is more about setting the direction, working out how to deal with whatever is
encountered and developing the capabilities to negotiate these by choosing people
with the right attributes for such a journey and equipping them with the required
skills. In strategic planning terms, the second organisation was preparing itself to
be agile, to be able to respond quickly as a unit to whatever it might encounter on
its journey. It has set a direction rather than a detailed route and has determined
the principles that will enable it to work out how to react (or how to proac-
tively take opportunities). And its strategy includes developing the capabilities to
succeed.

I have mentioned my reservations about the use of the term 'strategic planning'
and how its traditional stereotype interpretation can lead to perceptions of inflex-
ibility. The concept of a strategy journey, however, is capable of broader application encompassing the spectrum of circumstances and styles that might apply to
organisations.

We discussed in chapter 8 how an effective strategic plan is a platform for action.
It provides a reference that people can use to decide how to respond and a guide for
the organisation on its strategy journey. This might be a reference to the numbers that

Context (illustrative examples)	Stable competitive (e.g., grocery)	High growth specialised (e.g., technology)	Rapid change (e.g., digital)
Where are we now?	Analyse vs. competitors Consumer/trade trends	Understand strengths/ capabilities, position on technology map	Identify sources of change/ potential threats Analyse current strengths/ advantages
Where do we want to go?	Evaluate opportunities for advantage Cost efficiencies Strengthen brands	Target development opportunities Strengthen expertise/ capabilities in key areas	Scenarios re: possible futures Select areas for development focus (innovation/expertise)
How do we get there?	Selected initiatives (e.g., brands, costs, product development, trade relationships) Balanced investment	Explore target development opportunities (phased ventures) Develop system for identifying/evaluating opportunities	Develop focus areas Create organisational agility/ rapid 'assess and respond' culture
How do we make it happen?	Focus on themes/ initiatives Close monitoring of strategic measures	Manage investment in ventures/decision stages Frequent review of opportunities and audit of capabilities/expertise	Continually developing portfolio of high-energy projects (test-and-try) Test and improve agility to assess/respond

Figure 10.2 Strategic journeys

have been projected or the indicative timings for the various stages of a strategic development initiative; it could be using the rationale behind the model to rework these projections in the light of changes to the assumptions or in working out how to apply the strategy to a changing context. The organisation's understanding of the thinking by which this strategy was developed can help it to review whether that strategy is still the right choice if there are significant changes in circumstances to those on which the assessment of the organisation's situation was based originally – a different answer to the 'Where are we now?' question. And the principles and fundamental values that the organisation has articulated will be foundations to which anyone in the organisation can refer to guide his or her actions at any time during that strategy journey.

Organisational learning

One of the most powerful benefits of strategic planning is what is learnt by the organisation. An effective strategic planning process is a journey of discovery, when people come to a shared understanding about their organisation, its purpose and role, what they would like it to achieve and how it will develop to enable this to happen.

People also learn about strategic planning from their participation in this process – the technical aspects such as analysis and developing projection models, some of the tools such as 2-D grids and techniques such as using an iterative approach and developing a narrative. They can also learn more about how people think, the need to make sense of situations and how rich conversations help develop shared meaning. They will have seen the power of questions to drive the work in developing strategies, the value of asking 'What if . . .?' and the importance of constructive challenge. Thinking

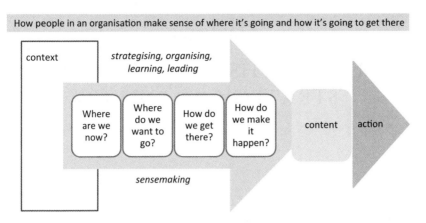

Figure 10.3 Strategic planning

through alternatives, evaluating options and making decisions can develop both individual and organisational abilities. Developing an effective strategic plan requires the synthesis of strategies and plans and the ability to adapt these whilst maintaining consistency. Especially powerful is learning how organisations can develop the capability to respond quickly to events using the foundations of the thinking they have developed together so far on their strategy journey. Undertaking such a journey will develop both people's individual skills and the organisation's capabilities in strategising, organising, leadership and learning and, most importantly, will strengthen their ability to undertake their next strategy journey adventure.

Epilogue

THE MATHS AND MUSIC OF
STRATEGIC PLANNING

Dry, complicated, remote, academic – many people's impressions about strategic planning are remarkably similar to the popular stereotypes about mathematics: that both are the domains of a few select experts who reside in ivory towers and produce work that provides little relevance to those who lead real lives and do the actual work each day. However, there is a tacit understanding that somehow mathematics is necessary to ensure that even everyday things work – and that from time to time it underpins some step-change in technology. But can the same be recognised for strategic planning?

Music, on the other hand, is about creativity, innovation, flair – and harmony, freedom of spirit and uplifting feelings; surely there are no similarities with the analytic-scientific mindset of strategic planning?

Yet strategic planning is, at its heart, about ideas, people and opportunities. It is how an organisation makes sense of where it's going and how it's going to get there. A strategic plan is how the organisation expresses its own story about itself and its desired future and how it will organise its resources to realise this. Beyond the stereotype perceptions, there are indeed similarities to both maths and music in strategic planning.

The mathematics of strategic planning is easy to see, on one level: numbers, analysis, organising and manipulating data, spreadsheets, formulae, projections, financial ratios and so on. But less superficially there is a more important similarity. Strategic planning uses a very mathematical way of thinking. A necessary condition for effective strategy development is to be able to drill down to the root of the situation, to develop a clear understanding about the real issue and to be able to tackle this problem from first principles. Issues need to be well defined, and this might require looking at the situation from different perspectives, developing models and concepts to help understanding and trying different approaches until you discover the right solution.

Strategic planning involves the consideration of options: working through various scenarios, testing hypotheses, evaluating the implications and assessing risks. There are aspects of linear programming too in determining the 'best fit' solution, the optimum balance between aspirations and resources. And developing a strategic plan often means working through several iterations, refining and improving, until the organisation reaches a sufficient level of confidence in a solution that it believes is the strongest plan to drive it forward.

As in mathematics, there is elegance in a good strategy. In every strategic planning process in which I have worked, there has been one important idea – a concept, expression, diagram, model or analysis – that has crystallised the thinking and enabled

120

the rest of the strategy development work and planning to flow. This is the one pivotal idea, the one chart or phrase that remains unchanged through the subsequent development and iterations leading to the final planning outcome. And like an elegant proof in maths (or indeed a defining chord or melody in music), once created a strategy can seem so simple, so obvious, so reasonable and so right that it belies the effort and the struggle involved in its development.

Strategic planning needs creativity and innovation, too – as does mathematics. The ability to search for new ways of looking at a situation, to try different approaches, to think around a problem until the solution becomes clear – all contribute to the development of an effective strategy and plan. And in creating strong, simple themes that express the essence of the story about the organisation's situation and the ideas about why and how it will develop, and then orchestrating how the various parts of the organisation need to work together to bring them to life, there are evident parallels with musical composition.

Like both maths and music, strategic planning uses a language, a means of expression that is understood by the people in the organisation. The roots of this and the notation are implicit, providing the axioms on which the thinking is developed and the shorthand by which it is interpreted. An organisation's strategic plan is the score, the directions and shape it will follow – and as in music, interpreting and delivering the score successfully is dependent on the players who perform it. There is scope for flair and improvisation, and the players in the organisation need to adapt to how the music flows rather than follow their individual parts slavishly – but at the heart of a successful 'performance' of a strategic plan is how well everyone understands the context and intention that lie within it.

Yet perhaps the most important analogies with maths and music take this to another level. In mathematics, the real value of developing a new proof, solution or technique is how this can then be applied in other situations. It provides a new way of looking at a problem, another approach and way of thinking that might lead to a solution. So it is with strategic planning. The thinking that has been applied in the process, the collective learning that both individuals and the organisation have gained: these are invaluable benefits they take forward and can apply to other challenges they will encounter. For me, this is one of the most powerful and rewarding benefits of working with the people of an organisation to help them develop an effective strategic plan – the knowledge, skills and experience they gain strengthen their ability to deal with the future.

Like music, an effective strategic plan shares the ability to inspire and to motivate. Just as music is about the sounds and harmonies that are played, and not just the score written on the page, so a strategic plan should be about what and how people in the organisation are doing every day, the encapsulation of shared core values and ambitions and a guide to decisions and action. It is how each player interprets the meaning behind the score as well as the notes, how thorough the understanding and how skilful the conductor in guiding and motivating each individual that distinguishes a great performance – and likewise a successful organisation.

So, strategic planning has depth and meaning within an organisation. Although the context for each organisation, the process by which it is developed and the style and detail of its content will vary, it is the combination of analysis and creativity, the maths and the music, involving the minds and the hearts of the people in the organisation, that ultimately make strategic planning so powerful, alive and relevant.

BIBLIOGRAPHY

Bridges W., *Managing Transitions: Making the Most of Change* (3rd edition), Nicholas Brealey Publishing, London, 2009

Gratton L., *Living Strategy*, Financial Times Prentice Hall, Harlow, UK, 2000

Hamel G. and Prahalad C., *Competing for the Future*, Harvard Business School, Boston, 1994

Johnson G., Scholes K., and Whittington R, *Exploring Corporate Strategy* (7th edition), Financial Times Prentice Hall, Harlow, UK, 2006

Kaplan R. and Norton D., *The Balanced Scorecard: Translating Strategy into Action*, Harvard Business Review Press, Boston, 1996

Kotter J., *Leading Change*, Harvard Business School Press, Boston, 1996

Kubler-Ross E., *On Death & Dying* (40th anniversary edition), Routledge, Abingdon, UK, 2008

Mintzberg H., Ahlstrand B., and Lampel J., *Strategy Safari*, Financial Times Prentice Hall, Harlow, UK, 1998

Porter M., *Competitive Strategy*, Free Press, New York, 1980

Stacey R., *Strategic Management and Organisational Dynamics* (5th edition), Financial Times Prentice Hall, Harlow, UK, 2007

Further Reading

de Wit B. and Meyer R., *Strategy Synthesis*, Thomson Learning, London, 1999

Grundy T. and Brown L., *Strategic Project Management*, Thomson Learning, London, 2002

Normann R., *Reframing Business*, John Wiley and Sons, Chichester, UK, 2001

Piercy N., *Market-Led Strategic Change* (3rd edition), Elsevier Butterworth-Heinemann, Oxford, 2002

INDEX

academic 7–9
agile organisation 117–18
analysis 7, 9–10, 23–5, 63–6, 69–70,
    109–10, 118, 120–1; Boston Consulting
    Group portfolio analysis matrix 68; PEST
    81; Porter's Five Forces 20; strategic
    analysis (tools, techniques) 1, 4, 67, 70;
    value-chain 20
assessment 36–8, 42, 48, 54, 112; risk
    see risk, risk assessment; situation 9–10,
    67, 74–6
assumptions 40–2, 74, 76; challenging,
    testing 63; checking, reviewing 114–15;
    projection models 77–9
Awayday 51, 55

Boston Consulting Group (portfolio analysis
    matrix) 20, 68

capabilities 10, 15–16, 49, 53;
    strategic planning 25
capacity 63–5, 79
challenge, framing the 43–6
change, managing 107
charts 63, 66–7
chess (analogy) 7, 53, 59
commitment 96–7, 100, 106, 108, 113–14
communication 28, 30, 46–8, 52, 70,
    96, 104
competence 8, 44–5, 106
competency 1, 44, 75, 87, 106
competition for resources 10
competitors 12, 15, 34–6, 40–1, 49–50, 75,
    78–9, 86, 115; competitive advantage 9
complexity theory 1, 97
consultants, management 9, 12, 20, 62, 74
context 15–19, 33, 38, 40–3, 61, 77–8, 86–7,
    95–6, 118–19
conversations 12, 26–7, 51–2, 55–6, 58–60,
    80, 96–9, 111, 114; rich conversations
    27–9, 48, 56, 60, 67–8, 95–6

corporate planning 9, 20
culture 10, 28–9, 98–100, 104; cultural
    web 95–9
customers 15, 59, 69, 72–4, 111–12

decisions 16, 18, 46, 54–6
deliberate strategy 35, 42
Drucker, Peter 98

emergent strategy 35, 42
energy, organisational 103–9

financial services 34

Gantt chart 108
GrandMet Brewing 73–4, 111
Gratton, L. 1
grid 66–9, 88, 118; predictable-control
    83; risk assessment (impact-likelihood)
    68, 84

Hamel, G. and Prahalad, C. 1
Harvard Policy Model (Harvard Business
    School) 8
healthcare 63–4, 81–2; NHS 34, 80–2
hypothesis 24, 74

insights 23–5, 62–6, 69, 80
intended strategy 40–2
iteration 56, 69, 120–1; iterative approach
    16, 27, 51, 58, 71, 118

Johnson, G. (Johnson and Scholes) 1, 98

key performance indicator 76

language 29, 66–7
leadership 13, 24–5, 28–9, 39, 41–2, 51–3,
    55, 59–60, 104, 115–16
learning 12–13, 24–5, 96, 99, 118–19
lifecycle (strategic plan) 38–9

management consultants *see* consultants
market 65, 68, 72–4, 76–9, 83–4, 86–7, 115;
  changes 40–2; environment 49–50; sectors
  36–7, 65
matrix 68
McVitie's 65
measures, strategic 108–12, 118
meetings 51–3, 58, 70
Mintzberg, H. 1, 8, 10

NHS *see* healthcare
NLP (neurolinguistic programming) 66, 72

options 48–9, 54–7, 59, 77, 79–80, 87
organising 22–5
ownership 95–8, 100, 106

PEST 80–1
planning cycle 40
Porter, M. 1; Porter's Five Forces *see* analysis
portfolio analysis matrix *see* Boston
  Consulting Group
projection models 77–9

realised strategy 40–2
rich conversations *see* conversations

risk 79, 83–5, 87; risk assessment 35,
  68, 84

scenario planning 20, 80, 82
Scholes, K. (Johnson and Scholes) 1, 98
schools of strategic planning 8–10
Scorecard, strategic 110
segmentation 65, 74
sensemaking 26–9, 95
Stacey, R. 1
strategic drift 10, 40
strategising 22–5
SWOT 38, 67–8
systems thinking 64

themes 17, 45, 84, 89–91, 105–11, 118, 121
2-D 66–7, 87–9, 91, 118

uncertainty 26, 60, 77, 80
United Biscuits 20, 65, 69, 74

values 72, 82, 90, 98–100, 118, 121

workgroups 58, 89
workstreams 49–50, 53–6, 58, 65, 71,
  89, 108